Stitch Zakka

22 Projects to Sew & Embellish • 25 Embroidery Stitches

Compiled by Gailen Runge

stash BOOKS.

an imprint of C&T Publishing

Text, Photography, and Artwork copyright © 2013 by C&T Publishing, Inc.

Publisher: Amy Marson

Creative Director: Gailen Runge

Art Director: Kristy Zacharias

Editors: Gailen Runge and Liz Aneloski

Technical Editors: Alison M. Schmidt and Amanda Siegfried

Cover Designer: April Mostek

Book Designer: Casey Dukes

Production Coordinator: Zinnia Heinzmann

Production Editor: Alice Mace Nakanishi

Illustrator: Mary E. Flynn

Photo Assistant: Mary Peyton Peppo

Photography by Christina Carty-Francis and Diane Pedersen of C&T Publishing, Inc., unless otherwise noted

Published by Stash Books, an imprint of C&T Publishing, Inc., P.O. Box 1456, Lafayette, CA 94549

Library of Congress Cataloging-in-Publication Data

Runge, Gailen, compiler.

 Stitch zakka : 22 projects to sew & embellish - 25 embroidery stitches / compiled by Gailen Runge.

  pages cm

 ISBN 978-1-60705-733-8 (soft cover)

1. Textile crafts--Japan. 2. Embroidery--Patterns. I. Title.

 TT715.R86 2013

 746.44--dc23

                    2012043754

Printed in China

10 9 8 7 6 5 4 3 2 1

Contents

Lecien Introduction

The earliest examples of embroidery date from ancient Egypt, Iron Age northern Europe, and the Zhou Dynasty in China. Initially embroidery was used to embellish items for high society. Young girls from wealthy families learned to embroider. By the late 1700s the popularity of embroidery had spread to the general population. Today embroidery is widely used to decorate a variety of items, including clothing, small personal items, table linens, and quilts.

Lecien was established in Japan in 1933 as an importer of French laces. In 1950 Lecien began to manufacture COSMO embroidery floss for the Japanese market. In 1979 the company began importing cotton quilting fabric from the United States. Twenty-one years ago Lecien began manufacturing original fine cotton fabrics and started selling them in the United States and other countries about ten years ago. The company began exporting its embroidery floss to the United States and other international markets in 2009. Today Lecien products are available in many countries around the world.

Lecien's COSMO embroidery floss is made from the best grade of Egyptian cotton available, and its texture and sheen are equal to that of silk. Due to specialized dyeing techniques, the floss has a superior level of color retention and does not deposit color on fabric. COSMO floss does not twist and tangle, and it easily separates into individual strands for stitchery projects. COSMO glides smoothly through the fabric and does not fray or knot during stitching.

COSMO floss is available in 443 colors, which were inspired by the changing seasons and other elements of nature. The wide range allows for subtle changes from one color to the next.

We want to thank all the designers who contributed to this book, and we hope you enjoy making these creative needlework projects.

—Art & Hobby Division, Lecien Corporation

Bird Family

An intimate group of feathered softies is a simple project, and ideal for either a first-time crafter or a more experienced sewer. With a small amount of fabric, felt, and thread, and a handful of embroidery stitches, this little family of birds will spring to life. I used patterned fabric from Lecien's Centenary collection by Yoko Saito; micro mini round buttons from Dress It Up; and light-weight paper or tracing paper for drawing the templates.

by Amy Adams of Lucykate Crafts

Finished sizes:
adult bird, 4½˝ × 3½˝;
baby bird, 3½˝ × 3˝;
egg, 1¾˝ × 2¼˝

Materials and Supplies

ADULT BIRD

- 5˝ × 12˝ piece of felted wool (or any fabric of your choice) for body

- 4˝ × 8˝ piece of craft felt for eyes, beak, chest, and wings

- 4˝ × 5˝ piece of print fabric for wings

- 4 small buttons for eyes and to attach wings

- Embroidery floss:
    Dark (COSMO #364)
    Light (COSMO #714)

- Stuffing

- Small pebble to weight bird

BABY BIRD

- 4˝ × 8˝ piece of felted wool (or any fabric of your choice) for body

- 4˝ × 6˝ piece of craft felt for eyes, beak, chest, and wings

- 2˝ × 5˝ piece of print fabric for wings

- 4 small buttons for eyes and to attach wings

- Embroidery floss:
    Dark (COSMO #364)
    Light (COSMO #714)

- Stuffing

- Small pebble to weight bird

EGG

- 3˝ × 6˝ piece of craft felt for egg

- 1˝ × 1˝ square of craft felt for decoration

- 1 small button for decoration

- Embroidery floss:
    Dark (COSMO #364)
    Light (COSMO #714)

- Stuffing

Embroidery Stitches

Buttonhole stitch   132

Lazy daisy stitch   133

Seed stitch   134

Straight stitch   134

Instructions

Template patterns can be found on page 137.

Birds

The adult and baby bird are made using the same process. The construction can be done by hand or machine. Use 2 strands of floss for all embroidery.

1. Trace all the template patterns onto paper and cut out on the traced lines.

2. Using the template from Step 1, cut 1 body from the felted wool; flip the template over and cut another body shape. Pin, right sides together, and sew around the edge approximately ¼˝ in from the edge, leaving an opening for turning right side out.

3. Turn the body right side out and stuff. Wrap a small pebble in stuffing and insert it at the base of the bird.

4. Use the templates to cut out the chest, 2 eyes, and a beak from the felt. Hold the chest piece in place, covering the open base of the bird, and sew it in place with random straight stitches using the dark embroidery floss around the outside of the stomach.

5. Add the eyes by sewing a button on top of a felt circle on each side of the head. Fold the beak in half and sew it in place with a few straight stitches in the fold (Figure 1).

6. Cut 1 wing from the print fabric; flip the template over and cut another wing. Cut 2 wings from the felt. Pin a fabric wing, right side out, to a felt wing and buttonhole stitch around the edge, using the light embroidery floss, to join the pieces. Repeat with the other wing.

7. For the adult bird's wings, embroider a flower in lazy daisy stitch near the top, using the light embroidery floss. Add a button to the center of the flower to attach each wing to a side of the bird (Figure 2).

For the baby bird's wings, embroider small random straight or seed stitches onto the wing area, using the light embroidery floss. Attach the wings to the sides of the bird with small buttons (Figure 3).

Figure 1

Figure 2

Figure 3

Figure 4

Egg

1. Use the template to cut 2 eggs from the felt. Decorate 1 piece with a flower in lazy daisy stitch using the dark embroidery floss. Add a circle cut from the craft felt, attached with straight stitches using the light embroidery floss, and a button in the center. Embroider some light and dark seed stitches randomly around the egg.

2. Pin the 2 felt eggs, with the embroidered side out, and sew around the edge in buttonhole stitch using the light embroidery floss. Just before you finish, insert a little stuffing into the egg and continue sewing to close the gap (Figure 4).

Wool Felting

There's no big secret to felting wool; it's more of a happy accident. First you need to find a suitable garment, which needs to be about 80% wool in content. Secondhand is the most economical way to go, so try thrift shops or yard sales, or raid your family's closets for any woolen sweaters, cardigans, scarves, and so on. To felt the piece, place the item in the washing machine on a warm wash / cool rinse cycle with some detergent and keep your fingers crossed! It doesn't need to felt very much, just enough to stop the wool from fraying when it's cut.

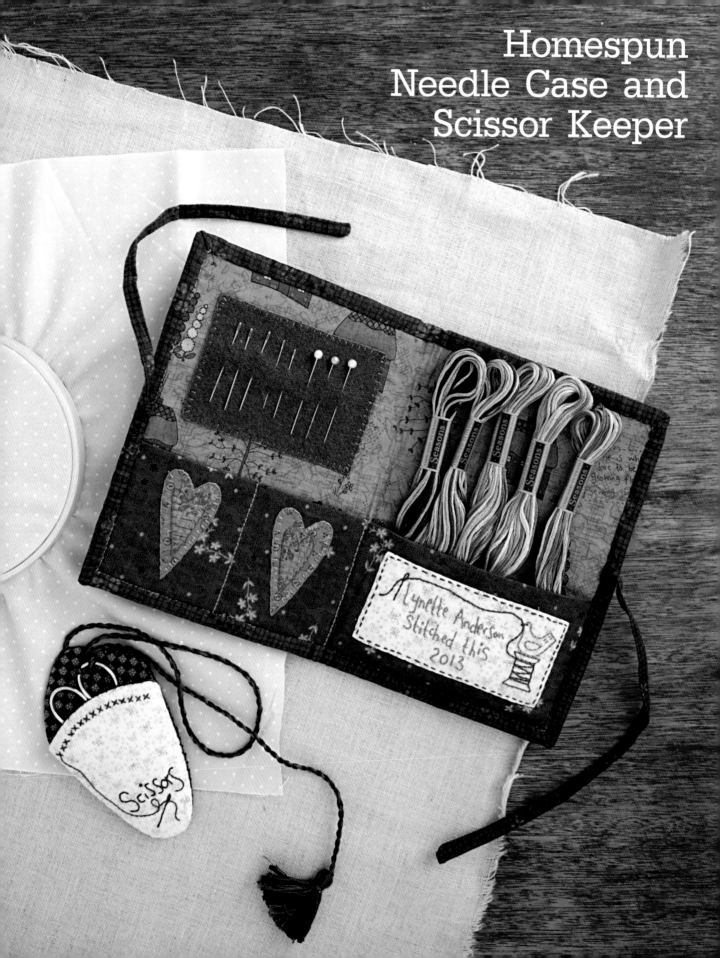

Make this needle case and scissor keeper for yourself or to give as a gift. It's a perfect heirloom to be treasured for years to come.

by Lynette Anderson

Finished sizes:
needle case, 4¾″ × 6½″ (closed);
scissor keeper, 2½″ × 4″

Materials and Supplies

NEEDLE CASE

- 6½″ × 9½″ piece of blue/brown print fabric for case exterior

- 6½″ × 9½″ piece of brown print fabric for lining

- 6″ × 10″ piece of off-white print fabric for embroidery background

- 5½″ × 9½″ piece of blue print fabric for inner pocket

- 2 strips 1″ × 10½″ of dark blue print fabric for ties

- 1 strip 1¼″ × WOF* of dark blue print fabric for binding

- Scraps: light blue floral, brown floral, and light brown floral fabric for prairie points and appliquéd hearts

- 2¼″ × 3¼″ piece of blue wool for needle holder

- 8″ × 12″ piece of heavyweight double-sided fusible stiff interfacing, such as fast2fuse (C&T Publishing)

- 4″ × 8″ piece of fusible web

- 4 small buttons

- Embroidery floss:
  Dark brown (COSMO #312)
  Light brown (COSMO #386)
  Dark blue (COSMO #735)
  Medium blue (COSMO #982)
  Charcoal (COSMO #895)

- Fine-tip fabric marking pen

- 6″ × 10″ piece of iron-on stitchery stabilizer (*optional*)

Embroidery Stitches

Backstitch 132	Lazy daisy stitch 133
Cross-stitch 132	Running stitch 133
French knot 133	Satin stitch 133
Herringbone stitch 133	

SCISSOR KEEPER

- 8″ × 8″ square of blue/brown print fabric for lining

- 5″ × 6″ piece of brown print fabric for back

- 5″ × 5″ square of off-white print fabric for embroidery background

- 5″ × 5″ square of iron-on stitchery stabilizer (*optional*)

- Embroidery floss:
  Dark brown (COSMO #312)
  Dark blue (COSMO #735)
  Charcoal (COSMO #895)

- Fast-drying craft glue

- 1 scrap about 6″ × 8″ of thin batting

- Card stock (I recycled cardboard from a cereal box.)

- Template plastic

- Fine-tip fabric marking pen

* WOF = width of fabric

Instructions

Template patterns can be found on page 139.
Embroidery designs are on page 17.

Needle Case
EMBROIDERY

Use 2 strands of embroidery floss, unless otherwise stated.

1. Transfer the embroidery designs onto the right side of the off-white fabric (see Transferring the Printed Patterns, page 130), using the stitch stabilizer if you prefer. Be sure to leave at least 1″ between the 2 designs.

2. Embroider the designs.

Dark brown:

Backstitch the sewing machine base.

Sew French knots for the birds' eyes.

Satin stitch the birds' beaks.

Light brown:

Backstitch the cat.

Satin stitch the cat's inner ear and the top and bottom of the thread spools.

Dark blue:

Backstitch the words *Needles and Pins*; the thread in the needles, on the spools, and in the sewing machine; and the solid line of the outer border.

Cross-stitch the X's.

Running stitch the dashed line of the outer border.

Charcoal:

Backstitch the measuring tape, the sewing machine, and both needles.

Using a single strand, backstitch the numbers on the measuring tape; the cat's eyes, mouth, and nose; and the chain between the collar and the heart.

Medium blue:

Satin stitch the heart on the sewing machine, the cat's collar, and the heart hanging from the cat's collar.

Backstitch the wording on the smaller design.

Outline the birds using backstitch. Outline the rectangle on the larger design in backstitch.

3. Sew the 4 small buttons to the stitchery inside the rectangle at the upper left corner.

4. Trim the needle case front design to 4″ × 5″ and trim the inner pocket design to 4¾″ × 2¾″.

5. Turn under the edges of each embroidered piece ¼″ all around, tack in place if desired, and press gently. Set aside.

NEEDLE CASE EXTERIOR

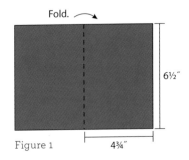

Figure 1

1. Fold and press the 6½˝ × 9½˝ piece of case exterior fabric in half as shown to mark the center so each side becomes 4¾˝ × 6½˝ (Figure 1).

2. Position the larger stitchery piece on the right side of the front of the needle case and pin in place.

3. Make 10 prairie points (see instructions below) and position them at the top and bottom of the stitchery, making sure the raw bottom edge of the prairie points is under the stitchery (Figure 2).

4. Stitch down the prairie points and the stitchery using a blind or invisible stitch.

5. Following the manufacturer's instructions, fuse the wrong side of the needle case exterior to the 8˝ × 12˝ piece of fusible interfacing. Trim the interfacing along the edge of the fabric.

Figure 2

Prairie Points

Cut 10 squares 1˝ × 1˝ from assorted fabric scraps. Fold, following the diagrams (Figure 3). Press after each fold using a hot iron.

Figure 3

INNER POCKET

1. Fold the 5½˝ × 9½˝ piece of inner pocket fabric in half lengthwise (Figure 4).

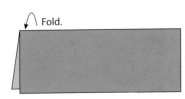

Figure 4

2. Fold and press the pocket in half to mark the center. Fold the left-hand end in to the center crease and press again to mark (Figure 5).

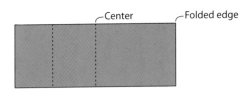

Figure 5

3. Trace 2 large hearts and 2 small hearts (page 139) onto the paper side of fusible web and fuse them to fabric scraps, following the manufacturer's instructions. Fuse a small heart centered on top of a larger heart. Fuse a double heart onto each left-hand section of the inner pocket (Figure 6), about ¼˝ below the folded edge. Using 2 strands of medium blue embroidery floss, buttonhole stitch around the edges of the appliqué shapes.

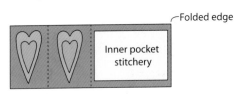

Figure 6

4. Using the photo (page 10) as a guide, position the inner pocket stitchery from Embroidery, Step 5 (page 12), and stitch in place invisibly.

NEEDLE CASE LINING

1. Pin the completed inner pocket on top of the 6½˝ × 9½˝ lining piece, both right sides up, aligning the raw edges at the bottom.

2. Using 2 strands of medium blue floss, backstitch on the crease lines of each pocket to divide them.

3. Pin the blue wool needle holder in place as shown.

4. Using 2 strands of light brown floss, buttonhole stitch around the edge of the needle holder to secure it. Gently press.

5. Fuse the assembled lining to the fusible interfacing side of the needle case (Figure 7).

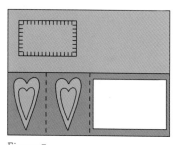

Figure 7

TIP

Use a tube turner to turn narrow tubes right side out, or follow the steps below, using a narrow piece of trim inside the strip of fabric:

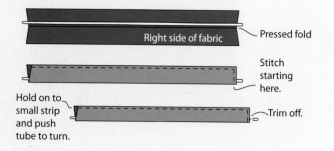

Right side of fabric

Pressed fold

Stitch starting here.

Hold on to small strip and push tube to turn.

Trim off.

Figure 8

TIES

1. Fold a 1˝ × 10½˝ strip in half lengthwise, right sides together.

2. Machine stitch across a short side and the entire long side (Figure 8).

3. Turn right side out.

4. Repeat Steps 1–3 with the other 1˝ × 10½˝ strip.

5. Pin the ties in place as shown (Figure 9). The ties will be stitched down when the binding is added.

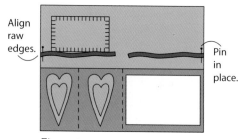

Align raw edges.

Pin in place.

Figure 9

BINDING

1. Fold a long edge of the binding strip ¼˝ to the wrong side and press (Figure 10).

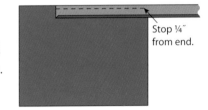

Figure 10

2. Align the raw, unfolded edge of the binding with the edge of the outside of the needle case. Pin in place along a side and stitch with a ¼˝ seam allowance, starting in the middle of a long side and stopping ¼˝ from the corner (Figure 11). Remove from the machine.

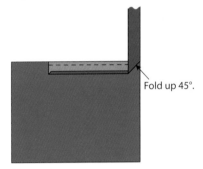

Stop ¼˝ from end.

Figure 11

3. Fold the binding strip as shown at the corner to allow the binding to ease nicely around the corner (Figures 12 and 13). Pin the next side and sew as in Step 2.

4. Repeat Steps 2 and 3 for all sides.

5. When you arrive back at the starting point, stop a few inches short of where you started. Refer to Binding Basics, Finishing the Binding Ends (page 136), to join the binding ends and finish attaching the binding. Your hand stitching on the opposite side should cover the machine stitching.

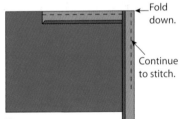

Fold up 45°.

Figure 12

Fold down.

Continue to stitch.

Figure 13

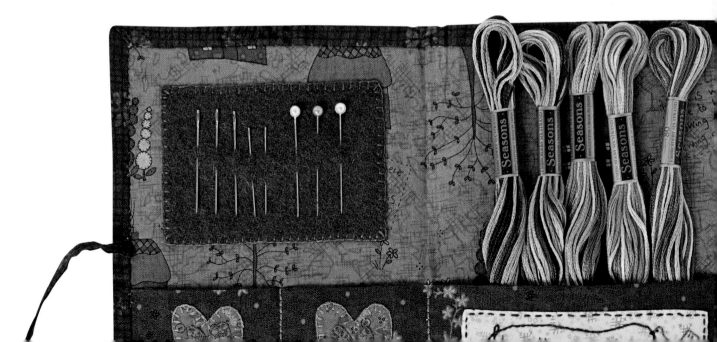

Scissor Keeper

EMBROIDERY

1. Transfer the embroidery design onto the right side of the off-white print fabric (see Transferring the Printed Patterns, page 130).

2. Embroider the design.

Dark brown:
Outline the wording using backstitch.

Dark blue:
Cross-stitch the X's.

Outline the thread in the needle using backstitch.

Charcoal:
Outline the needle using backstitch.

CONSTRUCTION

1. Make templates using template plastic for the scissor keeper front and back.

2. Trace the scissor keeper front template onto the wrong side of both the embroidered piece, referring to the project photo (at left) for placement, and the blue/brown lining fabric. Cut out these shapes approximately ⅜˝ beyond the drawn lines.

3. Trace the scissor keeper back template onto the wrong side of both the brown print fabric and the blue/brown lining fabric. Cut out these shapes approximately ⅜˝ beyond the drawn lines.

4. Trace a scissor keeper front and back onto batting and cut out *on* the drawn line.

5. Trace 2 scissor keeper fronts and 2 backs onto card stock and cut out *on* the drawn lines.

6. Glue a matching piece of batting to a card stock back and a card stock front.

7. Layer the trimmed stitchery front, right side down, and the batting / card stock front, batting side down (Figure 14). Glue around the edge of the card stock and wrap the excess fabric over the edge. Press in place while the glue is drying.

8. Repeat Step 7 with the card stock / batting scissor back and the brown print fabric scissor back, and with the remaining card stock front and back and the lining fabric front and back. Set all 4 pieces aside until dry.

> ## TIP
> To ensure that the embroidery is centered on the card stock, hold the embroidery up to the light with the card stock shape behind it. You will easily be able to see if you have it in the correct place.

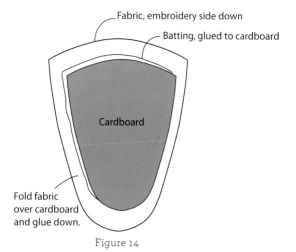

Fabric, embroidery side down

Batting, glued to cardboard

Cardboard

Fold fabric over cardboard and glue down.

Figure 14

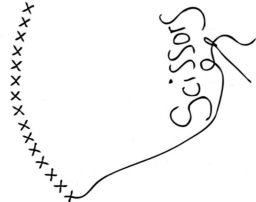

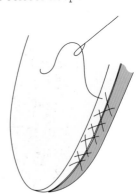

TASSEL AND CORD

1. To make the tassel, cut a piece of card stock 1¼˝ wide. Cut a length of dark blue floss and a length of dark brown floss, each about 30˝ long. Wrap both pieces of floss together around the card stock about 15 times. Start counting wraps from the bottom of the card. When the tassel is as large as you would like, carefully slide the loops off the card.

2. To make the cord, cut a length of dark blue floss and a length of dark brown floss, each about 48˝ long. Anchor the ends of the 2 threads under something heavy or ask a friend to hold the ends firmly. Twist the threads clockwise until the cord wants to double back on itself, but don't let it yet! Thread the twisted cord through the top loop of the tassel you just made, center the tassel on the cord, and now let the cord double back on itself. Hold onto the ends while it twists and then tie a small knot at the end to secure the cord. Cut through the bottom loops of the tassel. Take a short length of thread and wrap it around the tassel about ¼˝ from the top loop. Secure with a knot and bury the thread ends out of sight.

ASSEMBLY

1. After the glue has dried on the 4 pieces from Construction, Steps 7 and 8 (page 16), glue both front pieces wrong sides together. Hold the layers together with clothespins or binder clips while the glue is drying.

2. Sandwich the end of the twisted cord, centered, between the 2 back pieces, wrong sides together, and glue as in Step 1. You now have a back and a front for the scissor keeper.

3. Using 2 strands of dark brown floss and herringbone stitches, join the stitchery front and front lining pieces, along the top edge (Figure 15). Now, still using the herringbone stitch, join the front to the back, and continue stitching up and around the top of the back and back lining pieces to join them as well.

Figure 15

Three Pretty
Pincushions

*E*njoy stitching one or all of these pretty pincushions. Quick and easy to complete, these pincushions are the perfect project to keep for yourself or to give as a heartfelt gift. This is a great project to send to a friend across the miles; every time she stitches she'll think of you. All fabrics are from Lecien.

by Leanne Beasley
of Leanne's House

Finished sizes:
Sunshine Yellow Pincushion, 4¼˝;
Bonny Blue Pincushion, 4½˝;
Perfect Pink Pincushion, 6˝

Materials and Supplies

SUNSHINE YELLOW PINCUSHION

- 1 square 9˝ × 9˝ of yellow print fabric for pincushion front

- 1 square 9˝ × 9˝ of green print fabric for pincushion back

- Embroidery floss:
  Yellow (COSMO #144A)
  Pink (COSMO #204)
  Red (COSMO #241A)
  Green (COSMO #272)

- 2 squares 9˝ × 9˝ of thin fusible batting

- ½ yard of ⅞˝-wide yellow rickrack

- Fiberfill

BONNY BLUE PINCUSHION

- 2 squares 9˝ × 9˝ of blue print fabric for pincushion front and back

- Embroidery floss:
  Yellow-green (COSMO #269)
  Light blue (COSMO #523)
  Medium blue (COSMO #525)
  Aqua (COSMO #897)

- 2 squares 9˝ × 9˝ of thin fusible batting

- ½ yard of ¾˝-wide jade rickrack

- Fiberfill

- 2 buttons, ¾˝ in diameter

PERFECT PINK PINCUSHION

- 2 squares 11˝ × 11˝ of pink print fabric for pincushion front and back

- Embroidery floss:
  Pink (COSMO #204)
  Red (COSMO #241A)
  Lime green (COSMO #271)
  Orange (COSMO #753)

- 2 squares 11˝ × 11˝ of thin fusible batting

- ⅝ yard of ⅞˝-wide pink rickrack

- Fiberfill

- 2 buttons, 1˝ in diameter

Embroidery Stitches

Backstitch   132

French knot   133

Satin stitch   133

Instructions

Embroidery designs are on pages 22 and 23. All seam allowances are ¼″, unless otherwise specified. Use 2 strands of floss for all embroidery. For best results, use a hoop while embroidering.

EMBROIDERY

1. Transfer the embroidery design and the outermost circle onto the pincushion front fabric (see Transferring the Printed Patterns, page 130).

2. Iron the fusible batting onto the wrong side of the pincushion front and back fabrics, following the manufacturer's instructions and making sure to use an appliqué pressing sheet or Silicone Release Paper (C&T Publishing) to protect your iron and ironing board.

3. Embroider the design onto the pincushion front through both layers.

4. Press with a warm iron on the back, again using an appliqué pressing sheet or Silicone Release Paper on top of the fusible batting.

Sunshine Yellow Pincushion Embroidery

Backstitch the flower petals using red floss.

Stitch French knots in the flower centers using pink floss.

Backstitch the stems and leaves using green floss.

Stitch French knots in the background using yellow floss.

Bonny Blue Pincushion Embroidery

Backstitch the flower petals using medium blue floss.

Satin stitch the flower centers using light blue floss.

Backstitch the stems and satin stitch the leaves using aqua floss.

Stitch French knots in the background using yellow-green floss.

Perfect Pink Pincushion Embroidery

Backstitch the flower petals using pink floss.

Satin stitch the flower centers using orange floss.

Satin stitch the leaves and backstitch the center circle using lime green floss.

Stitch French knots between the flowers using red floss.

CONSTRUCTION

1. Cut out the pincushion front on the cutting line circle traced in Embroidery, Step 1 (previous page).

2. Using the pincushion front as a guide, cut out the back from the coordinating piece of fabric.

3. On the right side of the pincushion front, pin and sew a piece of rickrack around the edge (using a ⅛″ seam allowance), overlapping the ends and trimming the excess at the outside of the circle. *The side of the rickrack that faces into the circle when you pin will end up being the outside edge that is visible. Align the center of the rickrack about ¼″ in from the edge of the circle* (Figure 1).

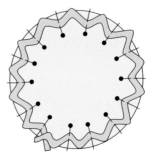

Figure 1

4. Place a matching pincushion front and back right sides together. Pin and stitch, leaving a small opening for turning and stuffing.

5. Clip the seam allowance all the way around between all the points of the rickrack; this is very important to prevent puckering. Turn right side out (Figure 2).

6. Press lightly with a warm iron. Stuff. Hand stitch the opening closed through all the layers.

Figure 2

ADDING BUTTONS

Start by stitching a button on the center top through all the layers, using coordinating embroidery floss. Once you have a few stitches holding the top button in place, add the button on the back of the pincushion in the same position. Stitch through both buttons a few times. This can be a little fiddly, so be patient. When the buttons are secure, knot the floss close to the fabric behind the back button, pull the needle through the fabric and out again, and trim the floss.

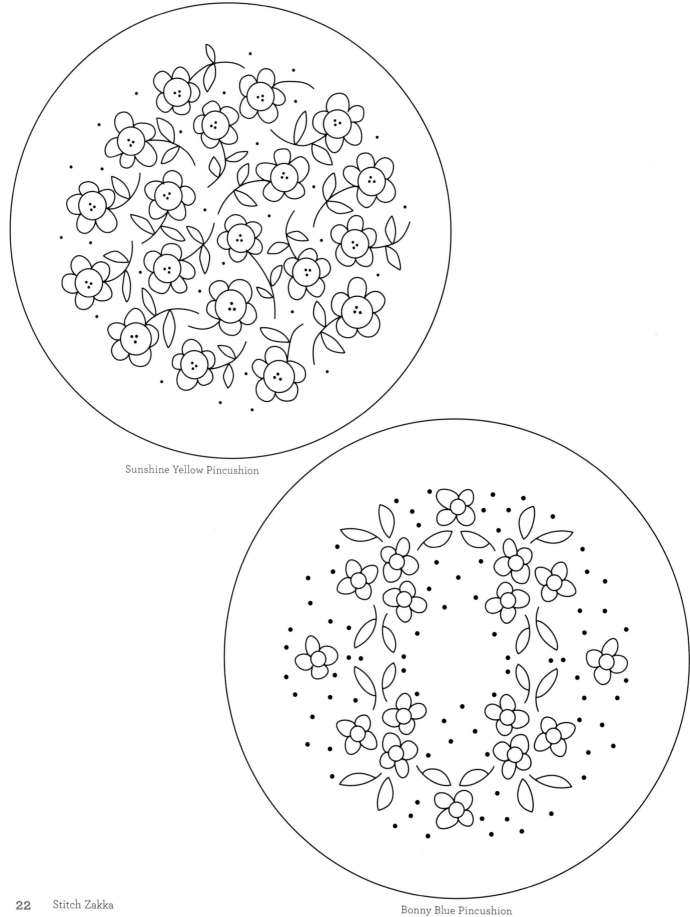

Sunshine Yellow Pincushion

Bonny Blue Pincushion

Perfect Pink Pincushion

Simple Sampler
Tablet Case

Block Tool

This design is a modern take on Victorian crazy quilting, which is typically chock-full of ornate fabrics and elaborate embroidery stitches. This toned-down version uses clean, straight lines and decorative embroidery stitches that are a little "fancy" in appearance but still fairly easy to execute. I also couldn't resist the juxtaposition of making a case for a high-tech gadget using the "old-fashioned" design elements of patchwork, embroidery, and hand quilting.

A mix of small-scale prints, solids, and tone-on-tone fabrics works best for this design, although a medium-scale print works well for the top strip. All fabrics used in the photographed project are by Lecien. Most are from the Petit Fleur collection. The light-colored tone-on-tone prints and linen are from Meg Hawkey's Whitewash collection.

by Kristyne Czepuryk of Pretty by Hand

Finished size:
10½″ wide × 13″ high × 1¼″ deep

Materials and Supplies

- 11 assorted fabric scraps each 12″ long and at least 4″ wide

- 1 fabric scrap at least 5″ × 5″ for clasp

- ½ yard of fabric for back, sides, and binding

- ½ yard of fabric for lining

- ½ yard of 45″-wide fusible batting (or regular quilt batting if you can't find fusible)

- 1 yard of 20″-wide fusible interfacing (*optional*; it just makes the case a little stiffer)

- 1 magnetic snap, ½″ in diameter

- Embroidery floss:*
  Light cream (COSMO #151)
  Medium blue (COSMO #2212)
  Medium purple (COSMO #282)
  Dark purple (COSMO #283)
  Light green (COSMO #316A)
  Medium green (COSMO #2317)
  Dark green (COSMO #318)
  Medium pink (COSMO #482)
  Dark pink (COSMO #483)
  Medium aqua (COSMO #563)
  Medium yellow (COSMO #701)

* Or use colors to coordinate with your fabrics.

Embroidery Stitches

Backstitch   132

Buttonhole stitch   132

Colonial knot   132

Cretan stitch   132

Cross-stitch   132

Feather stitch   133

Fly stitch   133

Herringbone stitch   133

Lazy daisy stitch   133

Running stitch   133

Stem stitch   134

Straight stitch   134

Cutting

ASSORTED FABRIC SCRAPS

Arrange the 12″ fabric strips in a pleasing order from top to bottom. Then cut the strips in the following widths (they will be sewn together in this order from top to bottom):

2¾″ × 12″	1″ × 12″	2″ × 12″
1½″ × 12″	1¼″ × 12″	1″ × 12″
1¾″ × 12″	1¾″ × 12″	1½″ × 12″
1½″ × 12″	2½″ × 12″	

CLASP FABRIC

2 pieces 2″ × 5″ for clasp

BACK/SIDE/BINDING FABRIC

1 piece 12″ × 15″ for back

1 strip 2½″ × WOF* for sides

1 strip 2″ × 26″ for outer binding

LINING FABRIC

2 pieces 12″ × 15″ for front and back

1 strip 2½″ × WOF for sides

4 *bias* strips 1⅝″ wide for seam binding

Side/bottom lining strip		
Bias strips for binding	Lining front 12″×15″	Lining back 12″×15″

Suggested cutting layout for lining fabric

FUSIBLE BATTING

2 pieces 2″ × 5″ for clasp

2 pieces 12″ × 15″ for front and back

1 strip 2½″ × WOF for sides

FUSIBLE INTERFACING

2 pieces 12″ × 15″ for front and back

1 strip 2½″ × 40″ (it's okay to cut this cross-wise as 2 strips 2½″ × 20″ and fuse each piece) for sides

* WOF = width of fabric

Instructions

All seam allowances are ¼˝. Use 2 strands of floss for all embroidery.

BODY FRONT AND BACK

1. To make the front, sew the 12˝ strips together (Figure 1). The pieced rectangle should measure 12˝ × 13½˝. Trim to measure 11˝ × 13½˝.

2. Complete the embroidery, starting at the top of the pieced rectangle.

Stitch Seam 1 (between the first and second strips) in buttonhole stitch using light green floss.

Draw a loopy line freehand through the center of Strip 2. Stem stitch on the line using dark pink floss.

Stitch Seam 2 in fly stitch using medium aqua floss and colonial knots using medium yellow floss.

Stitch Seam 3 in cretan stitch using medium blue floss.

Stitch Seam 4 in lazy daisy and straight stitch using light cream floss on the Strip 4 side.

Stitch Seam 5 in running stitch using dark pink floss on the Strip 6 side.

Stitch Seam 6 in feather stitch using medium purple floss and colonial knot using medium blue floss.

Stitch Seam 7 in lazy daisy stitch using medium green floss and straight stitch using dark pink floss on the Strip 7 side (Figure 2).

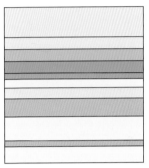

Figure 1

Figure 2: Lazy daisy and straight stitch combination

Figure 3: Backstitch and colonial knot combination

Stitch Seam 8 in cross-stitch using light cream floss on the Strip 8 side.

Stitch Seam 9 in backstitch using dark green floss and colonial knot using dark purple floss to create the flowers (Figure 3).

Stitch Seam 10 in herringbone stitch using medium pink floss.

3. Follow the manufacturer's instructions to fuse the 12″ × 15″ *fusible* batting piece to the wrong side of the embroidery, *or* baste the wrong side of the embroidery to the 12″ × 15″ *regular* batting piece around the outside. *Optional:* Following the manufacturer's instructions, fuse a 12″ × 15″ interfacing piece to the wrong side of the 12″ × 15″ lining piece.

4. Pin the embroidery/batting and lining layers wrong sides together.

5. Quilt as desired.

6. To make the back, repeat Steps 3–5 with the remaining 12″ × 15″ back fabric, batting, optional interfacing, and lining pieces.

7. Trim the quilted front even with the embroidered front fabric, and trim the quilted back to match (11″ × 13½″).

SIDES AND CLASP

1. To make the side/bottom piece, repeat Body Front and Back, Step 3, with the 2½″ × WOF strips of fabric, batting, optional interfacing, and lining. Trim this piece to measure 1¾″ × 36″.

2. To make the clasp, trace and cut out a paper template using the clasp template pattern (page 137). Trace the monogram (page 31) onto a 2″ × 5″ fabric piece as indicated on the template pattern and embroider the initial with backstitch (Figure 4).

3. Lay the 2″ × 5″ clasp fabric pieces right sides together. Pin the paper template to the pieces, lining up the straight edges at the top (Figure 5).

Figure 4

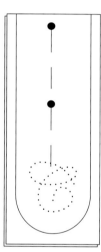

Figure 5

4. Sew around the template, just outside the paper, leaving the top straight edge open (Figure 6).

5. Trim the seam allowance to a scant ¼˝ (Figure 7).

6. Turn the clasp right side out and press.

7. Using the paper clasp template, cut out the shape from the 2˝ × 5˝ batting piece. Insert the batting into the fabric clasp (tweezers are helpful). Press again.

8. Embroider a running stitch ⅛˝ around the outside edge of the clasp in the same color as the monogram (Figure 8).

9. Following the manufacturer's instructions, attach the male side of the magnetic snap onto the wrong side of the clasp (Figure 9). Use the mark on the clasp template pattern as a guide for positioning the snap.

10. To make the inside binding, sew the 4 bias-cut strips together. Press in half lengthwise, wrong sides together. Fold the outer edges in to the center crease and press again.

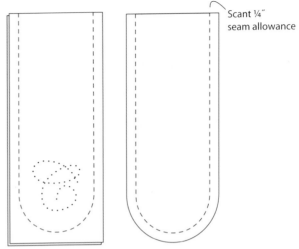

Scant ¼˝ seam allowance

Figure 6   Figure 7

Figure 8

Figure 9

ASSEMBLY

1. To attach the front to the side/bottom piece, mark the center of the bottom edge of the quilted front with a pin. Mark the center of the side/bottom piece with a pin. With right sides together, line up the pins, and then line up the rest of the bottom edge and the sides. Sew the front to the side/bottom piece.

2. Repeat Step 1 to sew the back to the side/bottom piece. Trim the strip ends even with the top of the front and back.

3. To finish the interior seams of the case, starting at the top of the case and working with the case inside out, align a raw edge of the bias binding strip, right sides together, with the raw edge of a side seam allowance. Pin in place and stitch by machine or by hand in the seam allowance, just past the outer fold of the binding so that the stitches won't be seen on the outside. Wrap the binding around the seam allowance, fold the pressed binding edge under, and stitch in place by hand (Figure 10).

4. Repeat Step 3 to bind the other interior side seam. Turn right side out and press the edges.

5. To attach the clasp, center it along the top edge of the back side, right sides together, and baste it in place (Figure 11).

6. Refer to Binding Basics (page 135) to bind the top edge of the case.

7. Following the manufacturer's instructions, attach the female side of the magnetic snap to the front. Position the center of the snap 1¼˝ down from the top edge (Figure 12).

Figure 10

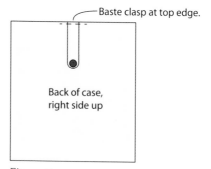

Baste clasp at top edge.

Back of case, right side up

Figure 11

Figure 12

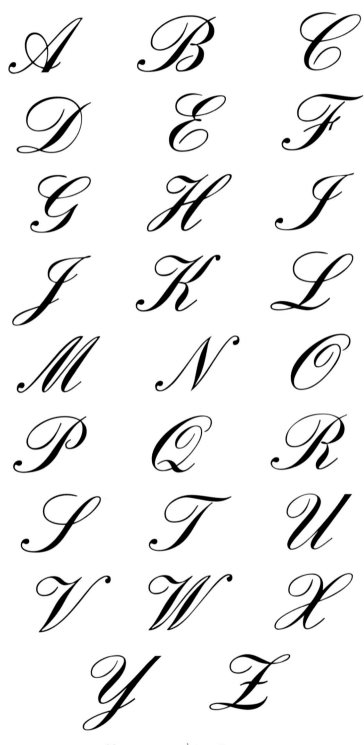

Monogram template patterns

Friendly Owl
Bookshelf Pillow

A cuddly pillow featuring a friendly owl who would love to keep your books company on the shelf, and perhaps read a few of them when you are not looking. I used Lecien fabrics from the Whitewash collection by Meg Hawkey and the Vintage Art Store collection by Susan Gower.

by Jasonda Desmond of Dotty Logic Design Studio

Finished size: 8″ × 9″

Materials and Supplies

- 9″ × 10″ piece of white fabric for pillow front

- 9″ × 10″ piece of print fabric for pillow back

- 9″ × 10″ piece of fusible interfacing, such as Shape-Flex (C&T Publishing)

- Embroidery floss:

    Brown (COSMO #312)

    Gold (COSMO #704)

    Light gold (COSMO #702)

    Gray (COSMO #368)

- Fiberfill

- 8 oz. of dried beans or rice

- Sandwich-size zip-top plastic bag

Embroidery Stitches

Satin stitch   133

Straight stitch   134

Instructions

EMBROIDERY

Use 3 strands of floss for all embroidery.
The embroidery design is on page 35.

1. Fuse the 9˝ × 10˝ piece of fusible interfacing, following the manufacturer's instructions, to the wrong side of the pillow front fabric to stabilize the fabric and prevent thread show-through.

2. Transfer the embroidery design onto the pillow front fabric (see Transferring the Printed Patterns, page 130).

3. Embroider the design.

Brown:
Straight stitch all the outlines.

Satin stitch the pupils of the eyes.

Gold and light gold:
Fill all the irises of the eyes and the buttons with satin stitch in gold. Satin stitch a few highlights in light gold.

Gray:
Satin stitch the eyebrows, beak, and claws.

Decorate the vest freehand with pinstripes (*optional*).

ASSEMBLY

All seam allowances are ½˝.

1. Place the embroidered pillow front and the print pillow back right sides together and pin.

2. Sew around the perimeter of the pillow, pivoting at the corners and leaving a 3˝ opening at the base.

3. Turn the pillow right side out and stuff lightly with fiberfill.

4. Open the plastic bag and place it halfway inside the pillow.

5. Using a funnel, fill the bag with beans or rice, zip it closed, and position it at the base of the pillow.

6. Hand sew the opening closed.

Rose Pillow Doll

With hands full of flowers and a pocketful of posies, this sweet embroidered design makes a simple pillow doll, perfect for any young girl. I used unbleached muslin and Lecien fabrics from the Antique Flower collection in Pastel and the Color Basic collection.

by Jill Hamor

Finished size:
4˝ wide × 10˝ high × 2½˝ deep

Materials and Supplies

- 16˝ × 16˝ square of cotton, muslin, or linen for doll front
- 8˝ × 12˝ piece of cotton print fabric for doll back
- 6˝ × 8˝ piece of fabric for doll dress and pocket
- ⅔ yard of fusible interfacing
- 6˝ × 8˝ piece of paper-backed fusible web
- Embroidery floss:
    Tan (COSMO #306)
    Red #1 (COSMO #800)
    Black (COSMO #600)

Dark brown (COSMO #312)

White (COSMO #2500)

Medium-dark brown (COSMO #311)

Dark pink (COSMO #3115)

Red #2 (COSMO #241A)

Medium-dark pink (COSMO #206)

Light-medium blue (COSMO #2412)

Light yellow (COSMO #141)

Lime green (COSMO #269)

Variegated pink (COSMO Seasons #8011)

Embroidery Stitches

Bullion knot   132

French knot   133

Lazy daisy stitch   133

Running stitch   133

Satin stitch   133

Stem stitch   134

Straight stitch   134

- Stuffing
- 1 yard of ⅜˝-wide trim (*optional*)
- 2 doll-sized buttons, ¼˝ in diameter (*optional*)

Instructions

The embroidery design is on page 39. All seam allowances are ¼˝.

DOLL BODY

1. Following the manufacturer's instructions, fuse interfacing to the wrong side of the fabric for the doll front. Repeat for the doll back.

2. Transfer the doll design to the right side of the doll front (see Transferring the Printed Patterns, page 130).

3. Embroider the doll design.

Tan:
Stem stitch the legs, arms, and face using 3 strands; the neck and knees using 2 strands; and the nose using 1 strand.

Red #1:
Satin stitch the mouth using 1 strand.

Black:
Stem stitch the eyebrow and eyelash lines using 1 strand.

Dark brown:

Satin stitch the irises using 1 strand of dark brown by bringing the floss from the center of the eye to the outer part of the iris. *(Hint: Leave the "highlight" area uncovered to better sink the white French knots.)*

White:

Add a small French knot highlight to each eye using 2 strands.

Medium-dark brown:

Stem stitch the hair using 6 strands.

Dark pink:

Stem stitch the rain boots using 3 strands and the hair ties using 6 strands. Add a French knot to a hair tie as a "knot."

DRESS AND POCKET

1. Follow the manufacturer's instructions to apply the paper-backed fusible web to the wrong side of the dress fabric.

2. *Making sure to reverse both shapes*, trace the dress and pocket shapes (separately) onto the paper backing. Cut out the dress and pocket on the drawn lines.

3. Peel the paper backing from the dress and carefully iron in place to the right side of the doll front. Repeat for the pocket.

4. Machine stitch around the outline of the dress and the pocket.

5. Machine stitch the trim to the hem of the dress (*optional*).

6. Outline the pocket, neck, and sleeve seams of the dress in running stitch using 3 strands of dark pink floss.

EMBROIDERY

Red #2 and medium-dark pink:

Use bullion knots and alternate between 6 strands of each color to make 3 roses (below the dress hem, at the pocket, and at the elbow).

Variegated pink:

Cut a few 12˝ lengths and use 6 strands of each (alternating for color effects) to make 3 more roses (a rose at the dress hem and 2 at the pocket).

Variegated pink, red #2, light-medium blue, and light yellow:

Embroider the remainder of the flowers using 6 strands of floss and a combination of lazy daisy stitches, French knots, and straight stitches. Refer to the embroidery design and photograph above for colors and stitches.

Lime green:

Using 3 strands of floss, add stems and leaves in stem stitch and lazy daisy stitch.

ASSEMBLY

1. Press the completed doll front, and trim ¾˝ from the embroidery to create the pillow shape.

2. Trim the fused doll back fabric to match the trimmed front shape.

3. Pin the doll front to the doll back, right sides together, adding lace or trim between the 2 layers if desired, and sew, leaving an opening about 3˝ on a side.

4. Clip or notch the curves as needed, turn right side out, and press gently.

5. Stuff the doll and close the opening with a ladder stitch.

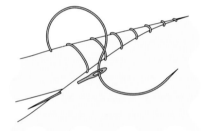

6. Secure 2 doll-sized buttons to the dress front (*optional*).

Party
Chicken
Project
Organizer

*U*se this handy project pouch to keep all your stitching supplies together when working on an embroidery project. The pouch has five pockets of various widths. The center pocket can be used to store a hooped-up embroidery, as hoops up to 8˝ in diameter fit easily. The pocket at the left can hold floss, and those on the right can accommodate scissors, a pencil, and a needle book. I used a Moda Bella Solid and Sew Stitchy by Aneela Hoey for Moda Fabrics.

by Aneela Hoey

Finished size:
9½˝ × 10½˝ (closed);
28½˝ × 10½˝ (open)

Materials and Supplies

- 12˝ × 30˝ piece of gray solid fabric for exterior

- ½ yard of red print fabric for lining and ties

- 11˝ × 29˝ piece of white print fabric for pocket

- 11˝ × 29˝ piece of batting

- Embroidery floss:
  Peach (COSMO #440)
  Yellow (COSMO #701)
  Orange (COSMO #758)
  Pale orange (COSMO #753)
  Dark pink (COSMO #206)
  Pale peach (COSMO #751)

  Medium pink (COSMO #353)
  White (COSMO #100)
  Pale pink (COSMO #351)
  Burgundy (COSMO #226)
  Aqua (COSMO #842)
  Metallic orange (COSMO Sparkles #6)

Cutting

RED PRINT FABRIC

11˝ × 29˝ piece for lining

2 strips 1˝ × 35˝ for ties

Embroidery Stitches

Backstitch	132	
Chain stitch	132	
French knot	133	
Lazy daisy stitch	133	
Running stitch	133	

Instructions

All seam allowances are ¼˝.

The embroidery design is on page 45.

EMBROIDERY

1. Transfer the embroidery pattern to the right-hand side of the gray solid fabric (see Transferring the Printed Patterns, page 130). Place it about 3˝ from the right-hand edge and 2½˝ from the bottom edge of the fabric.

2. Embroider the design.

Peach:
Outline the chicken body in running stitch using 6 strands of floss.

Make the leg tops with straight stitches using 6 strands of floss.

Yellow:
Make the beak with 2 straight stitches using 6 strands of floss.

Orange:
Make the comb in lazy daisy stitch using 6 strands of floss.

Backstitch the legs using 1 strand of floss.

Pale orange:
Backstitch the top wing using 3 strands of floss.

Dark pink:
Embroider French knots on the dots in the top wing using 6 strands of floss.

Pale peach:
Backstitch the middle wing using 3 strands of floss.

Medium pink:
Embroider French knots on the dots in the middle wing using 6 strands of floss.

Outline the tail feathers in chain stitch using 6 strands of floss.

White:
Backstitch the bottom wing using 3 strands of floss.

Pale pink:
Embroider French knots on the dots in the bottom wing using 5 strands of floss.

Burgundy:
Make a French knot for the eye using 3 strands of floss.

Outline the balloon string in running stitch using 2 strands of floss.

Make 1 cross-stitch at the chicken's leg using 2 strands of floss.

Aqua:
Backstitch the balloon using 6 strands of floss.

Metallic orange:
Backstitch just inside the head and tummy outline using 1 strand of floss.

3. Press.

TIES

1. Fold a red print strip in half, wrong sides together, along the length and press to crease.

2. Open out and then fold each of the long edges in toward the center crease (Figure 1). Press.

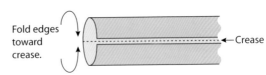

Fold edges toward crease.

Crease

Figure 1

3. Turn a short edge over by ½˝ to the wrong side (Figure 2). Press.

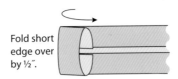

Fold short edge over by ½˝.

Figure 2

4. Fold in half along the length, so the 2 folded edges meet. Press.

5. Starting at the turned-over short edge, make a couple of backstitches and then topstitch down the length of the strip, a scant $^1/_{16}$˝ from the edge of the double folds (Figure 3).

Fold in half again.

Original crease

Figure 3

6. Repeat Steps 1–5 to make the second tie.

POCKET

1. Fold the pocket fabric in half lengthwise, wrong sides together. Press. Topstitch along the fold, ½˝ from the edge.

2. Place the lining fabric, right side up, on top of the batting. Position the pocket along the bottom with the topstitched edge toward the center of the lining. Pin and baste the pocket in position.

3. Make a mark 5˝ in from the right-hand side on the folded top edge of the pocket. Make a second mark 6½˝ in from the right-hand side. Draw a vertical line from each of these down to the bottom raw edge of the pocket.

4. Stitch along the 2 vertical marked lines, backstitching at the beginning and end of each (Figure 4).

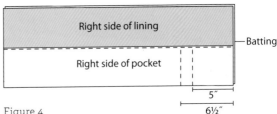

Right side of lining

Batting

Right side of pocket

5˝

6½˝

Figure 4

ASSEMBLY

1. Position the ties horizontally across the center of the pouch, with the raw short edges positioned just above the left-hand top edge of the pocket (Figure 5). Loosely knot and baste the ties in place along the left-hand side to keep them out of the way during the next step.

2. Trim the gray embroidered fabric down to 11˝ × 29˝, making sure to trim evenly from each side.

3. Place the exterior wrong side up on top of the right-side-up lining and pocket, so that the embroidery is at the left. Pin and baste through all the layers, all around the outside edge.

4. Stitch all around the outside edge, leaving a 6˝ gap along the bottom.

5. Turn right side out, making sure to turn the corners out well.

6. Hand sew the gap closed.

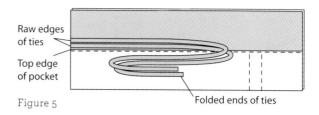
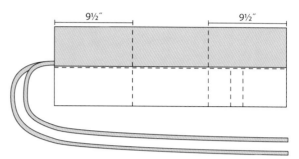

Raw edges of ties

Top edge of pocket

Folded ends of ties

Figure 5

Figure 6

7. Along the top edge of the opened-out pouch, make a mark 9½˝ from each of the sides. Draw a vertical line down from each mark to the bottom edge of the pocket.

8. Stitch along each vertical line, backstitching at the beginning and end (Figure 6).

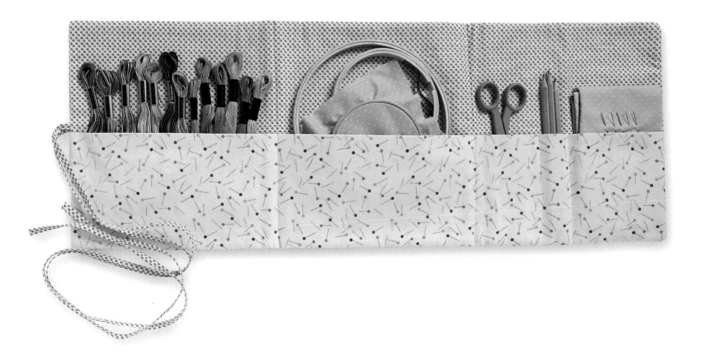

Instructions

Embroidery designs are on this page.

EMBROIDERY

1. Transfer the embroidery pattern for the clouds and 4 raindrops onto the white fabric (see Transferring the Printed Patterns, page 130), leaving at least 1″ between the shapes.

2. With right sides facing out, layer the light blue fabric, batting, and white fabric, and pin.

3. Embroider the design.

Dark teal:
Use French knots for the eyes and small backstitches for the mouths.

Teal:
Stitch through all the layers along the outlines using running stitch. Stitch around the outline a second time, again using running stitch, filling in the gaps. (This gives the look of backstitching but keeps the stitches looking the same on both the front and back.)

ASSEMBLY

1. Cut around each of the embroidered pieces, ¼˝ from the embroidery. Rub the edges a little with your fingers to encourage a bit of fraying.

2. Wrap the ¾˝ × WOF strip of blue fabric around the dowel so that all but the ends are covered. Secure both ends of the fabric with a small amount of craft glue.

3. Thread a length of crochet thread through the embroidery needle and tie a knot in the end. Stitch through only the batting layer at the top of a raindrop (Figure 1). Leaving about 4˝ of thread between the raindrop and the cloud, stitch through only the batting layer at the bottom of a cloud. Tie a knot to secure, and trim the end. Repeat with the remaining pieces so that each cloud has 2 raindrops, varying the distance between clouds and raindrops (Figure 2).

4. Using the same method as in Step 3, stitch through the batting layer at the top of a cloud and then tie the other end around the dowel. Repeat with the other cloud, varying the distance between the dowel and the clouds. Tie a doubled piece of crochet thread to each end of the dowel rod, forming a hanger.

Figure 1

Figure 2

Dream and
Bloom Redwork
Pillows

*S*titch this complementary pair of wonderful redwork pillows. They're sure to bring a bit of fun and whimsy to any space. The button embellishment is the perfect finishing touch.

*by Robin Kingsley
of Bird Brain Designs*

Finished size: 11˝ × 13˝

Materials and Supplies

- 1 fat quarter (18˝ × 22˝) of natural muslin

- ⅔ yard of red-and-white print fabric

- ⅓ yard of thin batting, at least 40˝ wide

- 8 buttons, ½˝ in diameter

- Embroidery floss:

   Red (COSMO #2241)

Cutting

MUSLIN

2 pieces 9˝ × 11˝ for embroidered redwork patch

2 pieces 5½˝ × 7½˝ for embroidered patch backing

RED-AND-WHITE PRINT FABRIC

4 pieces 11½˝ × 13½˝ for pillow fronts and backs

BATTING

2 pieces 5½˝ × 7½˝

2 pieces 11½˝ × 13½˝

Instructions

All seam allowances are ¼˝.

EMBROIDERY

Use 2 strands of floss for all embroidery, unless otherwise noted. Embroidery designs are on page 53.

1. Transfer the embroidery designs onto the 9˝ × 11˝ pieces of muslin (see Transferring the Printed Patterns, page 130).

2. Embroider the designs.

Dream:
Backstitch all the lines.

Use lazy daisy stitches for the loops.

Stitch French knots (wrap twice) on the dots in the flower centers and the berries at the top of the flower stem.

Add the bee's motion line with running stitch.

Satin stitch the bee's head and the large flower center.

Bloom:
Backstitch all the lines.

Use lazy daisy stitches for the loops.

Stitch French knots (wrap twice) on the dots. (For the dragonfly's body, use floss doubled in the needle—4 strands total.)

Add the dragonfly's motion line with running stitch.

Satin stitch the bee's head and the hollyhock flower centers.

> **Embroidery Stitches**
>
> Backstitch   132
>
> French knot   133
>
> Lazy daisy stitch   133
>
> Running stitch   133
>
> Satin stitch   133

EMBROIDERED SECTION ASSEMBLY

1. If needed, wash the finished redwork in warm sudsy water.

2. Rinse well, dry flat, and steam press, wrong side up, on a bath towel when the fabric is dry.

3. Trim the finished redwork piece to 5½˝ × 7½˝.

4. Baste a 5½˝ × 7½˝ piece of thin quilt batting to the wrong side of the finished embroidery.

5. With right sides facing, sew the embroidery and matching muslin backing together, leaving an opening at the bottom to turn.

6. Trim the corners, turn right side out, and press the edges.

7. Hand stitch the opening closed.

8. Repeat Steps 1–7 with the other redwork piece.

PILLOW ASSEMBLY

1. Baste a matching piece of quilt batting to the wrong side of the 11½˝ × 13½˝ pillow front piece.

2. Center the finished redwork patch on the basted pillow front, right side up.

3. Attach the redwork patch with a decorative button in each corner, tied on from the front side with thread doubled in the needle.

4. With right sides together, sew the basted pillow front to a pillow back, leaving an opening at the bottom to turn.

5. Turn right side out and press the edges.

6. Beginning and ending at the pillow opening, machine stitch 1˝ from the finished edge all around the pillow to make a flange.

7. Stuff the pillow and hand stitch the opening closed.

8. Machine stitch the remaining section of flange along the pillow's edge.

Little Deer Bag

*S*o off to the garden went little Ava. She was looking for her woodland friends and was delighted to meet the little deer and golden birds again; this was indeed her favorite place to be. The Little Deer Bag is a special tote bag for anyone who loves to dream. I used fabrics from the Woodland collection by Natalie Lymer for Lecien.

by Natalie Lymer of Cinderberry Stitches

Finished size:
10˝ wide × 11˝ high × 2˝ deep (excluding handles)

Materials and Supplies

- 6½˝ × 7½˝ piece of white linen for embroidery panel

- ⅓ yard of pink print fabric for bag exterior

- ⅓ yard of yellow print fabric for lining

- Embroidery floss:

  Yellow (COSMO #702)

  Gray (COSMO #2154)

  Medium cream (COSMO #382)

  Red (COSMO #241A)

  Green (COSMO #335)

  Charcoal gray (COSMO #895)

  Blue (COSMO #374)

  Variegated pink (COSMO #8008)

- ⅔ yard of 20˝-wide lightweight woven sew-in interfacing (I use Shapewell woven interfacing.)

- ⅓ yard of 45˝-wide fusible batting (such as Pellon Fusible Fleece)

- 6½˝ × 7½˝ piece of lightweight flexible fusible interfacing to stabilize the embroidery panel (I use Vilene H410.)

Embroidery Stitches

Backstitch 132

French knot 133

Lazy daisy stitch 133

Satin stitch 133

Straight stitch 134

Cutting

PINK PRINT FABRIC

2 strips 2½″ × 7½″ for front panel top and bottom sashing

4 strips 2½″ × 10½″ for front panel side sashing and bag sides

1 strip 2½″ × 11½″ for base

1 piece 10½″ × 11½″ for back panel

2 strips 2½″ × 15½″ for handles

YELLOW PRINT FABRIC

2 pieces 10½″ × 11½″ for front and back lining

2 strips 2½″ × 10½″ for side lining

1 strip 2½″ × 11½″ for base lining

WOVEN INTERFACING

2 pieces 10½″ × 11½″ for front and back

2 strips 2½″ × 10½″ for sides

1 strip 2½″ × 11½″ for base

2 strips 2½″ × 15½″ for handles

FUSIBLE BATTING

2 pieces 10½″ × 11½″ for front and back

2 strips 2½″ × 10½″ for sides

1 strip 2½″ × 11½″ for base

Instructions

All seam allowances are ¼˝.

EMBROIDERY

Use 2 strands of floss for all embroidery, unless otherwise noted. The embroidery design is on the previous page.

1. Transfer the embroidery design to the linen (see Transferring the Printed Patterns, page 130). Follow the manufacturer's instructions to fuse the 6½˝ × 7½˝ piece of lightweight interfacing to the wrong side of the linen.

2. Embroider the design.

Yellow:
Backstitch the birds' bodies and use lazy daisy stitch for the tail feathers.

Gray:
Straight stitch the birds' beaks and use satin stitch for the eyes.

Red:
Backstitch the toadstools, the ribbons around the deer, the pom-pom on the hat, the lips (1 strand), and the outline around the large round flowers. Backstitch the ribbon around the girl's neck; use lazy daisy stitch for the bow.

Satin stitch the spots on the deer and the gloves.

Outline the stockings in backstitch; use satin stitch for the stripes.

Place a French knot at the end of the tassel on the hat.

Green:
Straight stitch the grass.

Backstitch all the flower stems.

Satin stitch the spots on the dress and sleeves.

Gray:
Backstitch the deer bodies and the eyelashes (1 strand).

Satin stitch the girl's eyes and the eyes and noses on the deer.

Blue:
Backstitch the flower petals.

Backstitch the shoes; use lazy daisy stitch for the shoelaces.

Variegated pink:
Satin stitch the large round flowers.

Backstitch the dress, frills, and hat.

Medium cream:
Backstitch the arms, face, and nose, and the spots on the toadstools.

3. Press lightly.

BAG EXTERIOR

1. Sew the pink 2½˝ × 7½˝ strips to the top and bottom of the embroidered linen panel. Press the seam allowance toward the strips.

2. Sew the pink 2½˝ × 10½ ˝ strips to the sides of the embroidered linen panel. Press the seam allowance toward the strips.

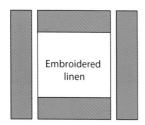

3. Pair the matching pieces of fusible batting with the pink print fabric pieces and the embroidered bag front panel. Fuse to the wrong side of the fabric, following the manufacturer's instructions.

4. Baste the woven interfacing pieces to the wrong side of the fused pieces to add stability to the bag.

5. Stitch in-the-ditch around the outside of the embroidery panel.

6. Sew the remaining pink 2½˝ × 10½˝ side strips to each side of the embroidered front panel.

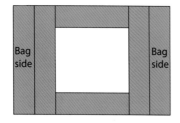

7. Sew the assembled front/side section and back panel together to form a tube. Turn right side out, press, and topstitch along the length of each corner seam.

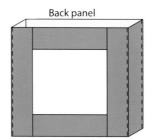

Topstitch along 4 corner seams.

8. Turn the bag wrong side out again and pin the 2½˝ × 11½˝ base piece along the bottom edge of the bag tube, sewing the front and back (longer) seams first.

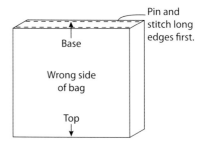

9. Pin and sew the (short) side seams and turn the bag right side out. Press lightly and topstitch along the front and back seam at the bottom of the bag.

BAG LINING

1. Sew a yellow print 2½˝ × 10½˝ side lining piece to either side of the yellow print 10½˝ × 11½˝ front lining piece.

2. Repeat Bag Exterior, Steps 7 and 8, leaving a 4˝ opening in a long seam for the finishing steps, but don't topstitch any of the lining seams.

BAG HANDLES

1. Fold 2 interfaced handle strips in half, right sides together, along the length and sew. Turn right side out and press the seam to the side. Double topstitch the handle along both long edges.

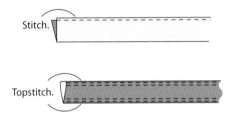

2. Baste the handles 3˝ from the side seams, matching the raw edges.

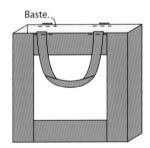

FINISHING

1. With right sides together, place the bag exterior inside the bag lining, match the side seams, and pin.

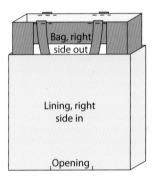

2. Stitch the top edge, turn right side out through the opening left in the lining, and slipstitch the opening closed.

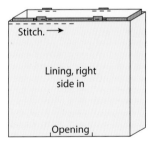

3. Push the lining into the bag, press the top edge, and double topstitch to complete.

Daisy Place Mat
and Napkin

Whether you make one set or a whole collection, these place mats and napkins will make your table look perfect. Change the floss colors and fabrics to match any decor. This is the perfect solution for that special gift you've been trying to find. I used Walnut Hill Farm by Charlotte Lyons for Blend Fabrics.

by Charlotte Lyons

Finished sizes:
place mat, 16″ × 11″;
napkin, 19″ × 19″

Materials and Supplies

- ⅜ yard of linen fabric for place mat

- 12″ × 17″ piece of yellow fabric for place mat

- 20″ × 20″ square of green fabric for napkin

- Water-soluble fabric marker

- Embroidery floss:
    Yellow (COSMO #302)
    Light yellow (COSMO #700)
    Orange (COSMO #146)
    Green (COSMO #632)
    Light green (COSMO #671)

Embroidery Stitches

Backstitch	132
Chain stitch	132
French knot	133

Cutting

LINEN

1 piece 6″ × 12″ for embroidered panel

1 piece 12″ × 17″ for place mat backing

Instructions

All seam allowances are ½˝, unless otherwise noted.

EMBROIDERY

Use 3 strands of floss for all embroidery. The embroidery design is on page 61.

1. Use a water-soluble marker to transfer the design to the 6˝ × 12˝ linen panel (see Transferring the Printed Patterns, page 130).

2. Embroider the design.

Yellow:
Backstitch the flower's outline.

Light yellow:
Fill the flower petals using chain stitch.

Orange:
Fill the flower center with chain stitch.

Green:
Chain stitch the stem and leaves.

Light green:
Chain stitch the vase and make French knots for the dots inside the vase.

PLACE MAT ASSEMBLY

1. Fold the raw edges of the long sides of the embroidered linen panel under by ¾˝ and press to create a panel 4½˝ × 12˝.

2. Pin this panel to the right side of the 12˝ × 17˝ yellow piece, 4˝ from the left-hand edge. Topstitch along the edges of the linen on the left and right sides (Figure 1).

3. Pin the 12˝ × 17˝ linen place mat back and assembled place mat top right sides together.

4. Sew around the edges, leaving an opening for turning on the bottom (Figure 2).

5. Trim the corners and turn right side out. Press, taking care to fold in the seam allowances at the opening.

6. Topstitch all the way around, closing the opening.

NAPKIN

1. Fold each edge of the 20˝ × 20˝ square of green fabric under by ¼˝ twice to the wrong side, pressing after each fold, and pin in place (Figure 3).

2. Topstitch around all 4 sides close to the inner fold. Press.

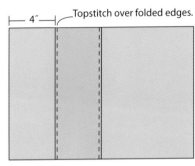

Figure 1

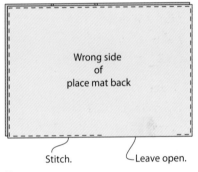

Figure 2

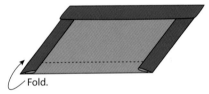

Figure 3

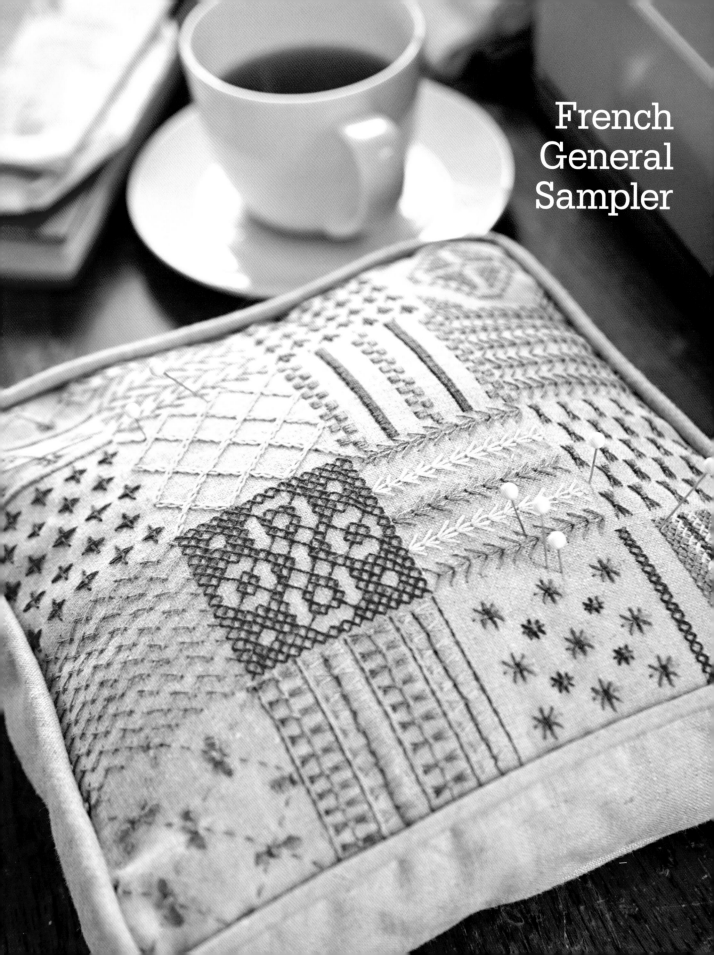

French
General
Sampler

This is the ideal decorative sampler to make when you want to learn or perfect your stitches. Use it as a pincushion, small pillow, or cushion. Just change the colors for the perfect addition to any decor.

by Kaari Meng of French General

Finished size:
8″ wide × 8″ high × 2″ deep

Materials and Supplies

- ⅝ yard of linen fabric

- 2¼ yards of ¼″ cord for piping

- Embroidery floss:
  Light red #1 (COSMO #464)
  Light red #2 (COSMO #855)
  Red (COSMO #858)
  Bright red (COSMO #346)
  Dark red #1 (COSMO #108)
  Light blue (COSMO #163)
  Light-medium blue (COSMO #164)
  Medium blue (COSMO #733)
  Medium-dark blue (COSMO #734)
  Light gray (COSMO #712)
  Medium gray (COSMO #715)
  Dark gray (COSMO #893)

- Fiberfill

- 1 cup of ground walnut shells

Embroidery Stitches

Butterfly chain stitch 132	Satin stitch 133
Chain stitch 132	Sheaf stitch 134
Cross-stitch 132	Star stitch 134
Feather stitch 133	Stem stitch 134
Fern stitch 133	Tulip stitch 134
French knot 133	Wheat ear stitch 134
Herringbone stitch 133	Woven cross stitch 134

Cutting

LINEN

2 squares 8½″ × 8½″

4 pieces 2½″ × 8½″

4 bias strips 2½″ wide

CORD

2 pieces 40″ long

Book Tree
e-Reader Case

I *love embroidery over patterned fabrics; it makes a real impact and gives a traditional craft a contemporary feel. I have used this technique to create a cute slipcase for a Kindle. It's a very simple project featuring easy-to-master embroidery stitches, so why not give it a go?*

by Lisa Neal of Lazy May

Finished size: 5˝ × 7˝

Materials and Supplies

- 4 pieces 6˝ × 8˝ of baby pink polka-dot print canvas

- 2 pieces 5˝ × 7˝ of felt

- Embroidery floss:
    Bright pink (COSMO #203)

- 5˝ × 7˝ piece of cardboard or template plastic

Embroidery Stitches

Backstitch   132

Split stitch   134

Stem stitch   134

Instructions

All seam allowances are ½˝. The embroidery design is on page 71.

EMBROIDERY

1. Transfer the design onto a piece of print canvas (see Transferring the Printed Patterns, page 130).

2. Embroider the design.

Stem stitch the tree and foliage using 4 strands of floss.

Split stitch the girl's dress using 3 strands of floss.

Stem stitch the girl's body and the books using 2 strands of floss.

Backstitch the girl's face and the book titles and ribbons using 2 strands of floss.

CONSTRUCTION

1. Center the 5″ × 7″ template on the wrong side of the completed embroidery and trace around it with a pencil; hold the fabric up to the light to ensure that the embroidery has been framed evenly by the pencil line.

2. Pin a second piece of canvas to the embroidered piece, right sides together, and stitch on the drawn line *only* where indicated. Start ½″ down from the top of the case, backstitching at the beginning of the seam, pivoting at the top 2 corners, and backstitching at the end of the seam ½″ down from the top on the other side (Figure 1).

3. Trim the corners and the top seam allowance to reduce bulk (Figure 2). Turn the piece right side out and press.

4. Tuck a piece of felt inside the stitched top section. It should lie flat and butt up to the top seam neatly. Pin in place.

5. Repeat Steps 1–4 with the remaining 2 pieces of polka-dot fabric to finish the top edge of the other half of the case.

6. Lay the 2 halves on top of each other, with the embroidery facing in and the already-sewn top edges aligned, and pin. The case is now pinned right sides together.

7. Place the 5″ × 7″ template on top of the case, lining it up with the top seams and corners, and draw around it with a pencil.

8. Stitch the 2 halves together securely on the drawn line (Figure 3). You will be stitching through 4 layers of canvas, encasing the felt pieces in each half. Trim the raw edges and corners to reduce bulk and turn right side out.

9. Press with a hot iron and you're done!

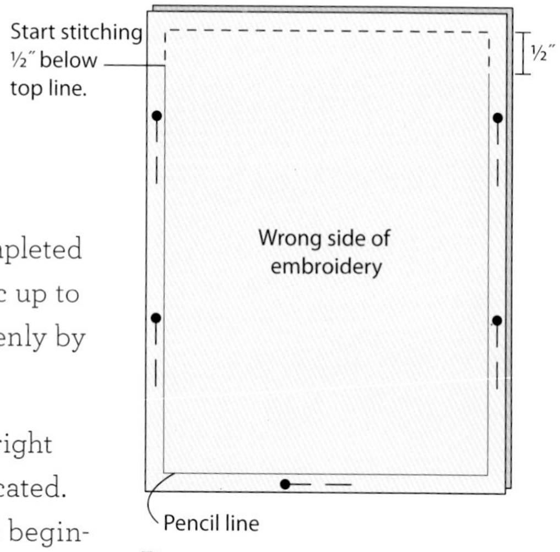

Start stitching ½″ below top line.

½″

Wrong side of embroidery

Pencil line

Figure 1

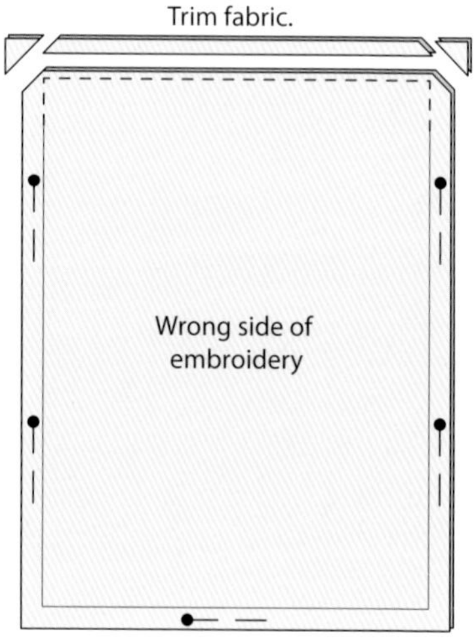

Trim fabric.

Wrong side of embroidery

Figure 2

Stitch along drawn line.

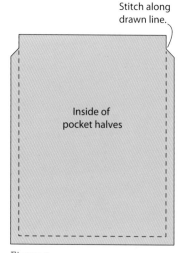

Inside of pocket halves

Figure 3

Springtime
Stitchery

A waken springtime with this fun, cheerful design. It's sure to brighten any special corner of your house.

*by Rosalie Quinlan
of Rosalie Quinlan Designs*

Finished size: 10˝ × 12˝ (framed)

Materials and Supplies

- 14˝ × 14˝ square of cream-colored linen

- 2 strips 4½˝ × 10˝ and 2 strips 4½˝ × 16½˝ of teal print fabric for borders

- 14˝ × 14˝ square of thin fusible woven interfacing, such as Shape-Flex (by C&T Publishing)

- Embroidery floss:

    Light pink (COSMO #113)

    Dark pink (COSMO #2114)

    Light jade (COSMO #897)

    Jade (COSMO #899)

    Light purple (COSMO #173)

    Purple (COSMO #175)

    Orange (COSMO #444)

    Yellow (COSMO #700)

    Red (COSMO #800)

- 10˝ × 12˝ artist's canvas (*optional*)

Embroidery Stitches

Backstitch   132

Chain stitch   132

Satin stitch   133

Instructions

EMBROIDERY

Use 2 strands of floss for all embroidery, unless noted otherwise. The embroidery design is on page 75.

1. Transfer the design onto the linen fabric (see Transferring the Printed Patterns, page 130).

2. Iron thin fusible woven interfacing to the entire back of the work to prevent threads from showing through.

3. Refer to the finished project photo (page 73) for color placement, and embroider the design.

Make French knots for the birds' eyes, using a single strand of floss.

Backstitch the thin lines using a single strand of floss. Outline the birds' wings with running stitches.

Use tiny chain stitches for the thicker lines and to fill in the 2 hearts.

Satin stitch to fill in the remaining circles, scallops, and teardrops.

FINISHING

1. Trim the stitchery to measure 8½˝ × 10½˝. Be very careful to center the design when you cut.

2. Sew a 4½˝ × 10½˝ strip of border fabric to each side of the stitchery. Press the seam allowances open.

3. Sew 4½˝ × 16½˝ strips of border fabric to the top and bottom of the stitchery. Press the seam allowances open.

4. Center and stretch the stitchery around a 10˝ × 12˝ artist's canvas, or frame it. Use a staple gun at the back of the canvas to hold the stitchery in place.

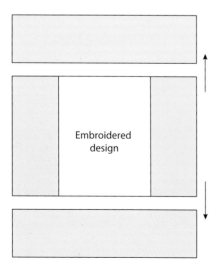

Embroidered design

Spring Baskets Wallhanging

The inspiration for this design evolved as I was looking at old-timey quilt blocks and poking around antique stores. I love vintage embroidered linens. In this wall-hanging, the baskets are like pieced blocks and the black thread reminds me of old stitchery. The funky leaves and flowers are more modern. This quilt offers something old and something new. Fabrics are from the Antique Flower collection in Pastel by Lecien.

by Judy Reynolds
of Black Cat Creations

Finished size:
block, 6˝ × 6˝;
quilt, 30˝ × 30˝

Materials and Supplies

- ½ yard of white fabric for embroidered colored blocks

- 4 different fat eighths of polka-dot fabric for corner blocks (Template A)

- 4 different fat eighths of large floral print fabric for corner blocks (Template A)

- 4 different fat quarters of medium floral print fabric for inner and outer borders

- 4 different fat quarters of small floral print fabric for center block and outer border

- 1 fat quarter (or ⅓ yard) of large light floral print fabric for inner border

- ⅔ yard of black print fabric for inner and outer borders

- 1 yard of backing fabric

- ⅓ yard of binding fabric

- 34˝ × 34˝ square of batting

- Piece of muslin for heat setting the crayon

- Embroidery floss:
    Pink (COSMO #113)
    Dark green (COSMO #120)
    Salmon (COSMO #186)
    Light teal (COSMO #373)
    Aqua (COSMO #372)
    Dark teal (COSMO #374)
    Blue (COSMO #525)
    Sage green (COSMO #535)
    Black (COSMO #600)
    Green (COSMO #633)
    Yellow (COSMO #701)
    Dark yellow (COSMO #702)
    Rose (COSMO #2222)
    Dark pink (COSMO #2223)
    Teal (COSMO #2563)
    Olive green (COSMO #2631)

> **Embroidery Stitches**
>
> Backstitch   132
>
> French knot   133
>
> Running stitch   133

- Card stock or template plastic

- Freezer paper

- Permanent fine-point pen

- Box of 96 Crayola crayons

- 16 buttons, diameters varying from 5/16˝ to ½˝

Cutting

Template patterns can be found on pages 86 and 87. Copy and trace the template patterns for Template A and the large and small yo-yos onto card stock or template plastic and cut out on the drawn lines.

WHITE FABRIC

4 squares 9˝ × 9˝ for embroidered colored blocks (Blocks 1–4)

1 square 6˝ × 6˝ for center block (Block 5)

POLKA-DOT FABRICS

1 square 8˝ × 8˝ from each fat eighth for embroidered corner blocks

LARGE FLORAL PRINT FABRICS

1 of Template A from each fat eighth for embroidered corner blocks

MEDIUM FLORAL PRINT FABRICS

1 square 5⅜˝ × 5⅜˝ from each fat quarter, then cut once diagonally for inner border (You will use only 1 triangle from each fabric.)

1 square 3⅞˝ × 3⅞˝ from each fat quarter, then cut once diagonally for outer border corners (You will use only 1 triangle from each fabric.)

8 pieces 2˝ × 3½˝ from each fat quarter for outer border

SMALL FLORAL PRINT FABRICS

2 squares 4¼˝ × 4¼˝ from 1 fabric, then cut each once diagonally for center block

8 pieces 2˝ × 3½˝ from each fat quarter for outer border

LARGE LIGHT FLORAL PRINT FABRIC

8 strips 2½˝ × 15˝ for inner border

BLACK PRINT FABRIC

8 strips 1½˝ × 15˝ for inner border

2 squares 3⅞˝ × 3⅞˝, then cut once diagonally for outer border corners

3 strips 2˝ × WOF,* then cut into 64 squares 2˝ × 2˝

VARIOUS FABRICS/SCRAPS FROM CUTTING

4 large circles for yo-yos

12 small circles for yo-yos

BINDING FABRIC

4 strips 2½˝ × WOF

* WOF = width of fabric

Block 1 (top center)

Block 2 (middle right)

Block 3 (bottom center)

Instructions

Embroidery designs are on pages 86–89.

COLORED BLOCKS

1. Press the shiny side of freezer paper to the back side of the background fabric. This will keep the fabric from moving around while you are tracing and coloring.

2. Transfer the designs for Blocks 1–5 onto the white 9˝ × 9˝ squares (see Transferring the Printed Patterns, page 130).

Block 4 (middle left)

Block 5 (center)

3. Color lightly with the first color listed, to provide a base for each area. Lay a piece of muslin over the colored area; heat set using a hot, dry iron (cotton setting); and then add more color (using the suggested shading colors listed below). Heat set after each application of crayon color.

4. Remove freezer paper.

TIP

If the color listed is not in your crayon box, refer to the photograph (page 79) and substitute an appropriate color.

Block number	Crayon color*	Area
Block 1	Carnation pink/wild strawberry	Basket handle, top row triangles, zigzag with dots
	Wild strawberry/jazzberry jam	Zigzag with stripes
	Green	Leaves
	Olive green/green-yellow	Leaf edges
	Dandelion	Flower edges
	Dandelion/orange	Flower centers, polka dots
Block 2	Sky blue/aquamarine	Basket handle, 5 squares
	Sky blue	Triangles in basket
	Dandelion	Half-star in basket, flower centers
	Carnation pink	Polka dots
	Carnation pink/pink flamingo/wild strawberry	Flowers
	Fern green (top), olive green (bottom)	Leaves
Block 3	Dandelion	Basket handle, flower centers, outer and inner center triangles
	Sky blue/aquamarine/cornflower	Large flowers
	Carnation pink/wild strawberry	Small flowers, triangles, squares in basket
	Green (outside edge), olive green (center)	Leaves
Block 4	Green	Basket handle, dotted triangles
	Fern green	Striped areas in basket
	Carnation pink/jazzberry jam	Flowers
	Dandelion (center), orange (outer edge)	Flower centers
	Olive green	Leaves

Blend the multiple colors as noted: carnation pink/wild strawberry

EMBROIDERY

Use 3 strands of floss for colored stitching and 2 strands for black stitching.

Use backstitch, French knots, or running stitch to embroider the design as indicated; all straight lines are backstitch.

Block 1

Dark pink: basket, handle, zigzag outline and stripes

Rose: dashes in handle and in triangles in basket

Dark yellow: outer flower petals

Salmon: centers of flower petals

Green: inner leaves

Olive green: outer edges of leaves

Black: polka dots, leaf veins and X's, stems, flower stamens

Block 2

Dark teal: basket, handle outline, striped blocks

Yellow: half-star in basket, flower centers, single French knots around flower centers, tiny flowers

Blue: dashes in basket triangles, stripes on handle

Rose: outer row of stitching on large flowers

Pink: inner row of stitching on large flowers and French knots in centers of tiny flowers

Sage green: leaves (top and veins)

Olive green: leaves (bottom and veins)

Black: polka dots, stems, leaf center vein

Block 3

Dark yellow: basket, handle, dashes in handle and triangles, basket center triangles

Yellow: basket squares, triangles with dots, single French knots in triangles, large flower centers, single French knots in centers of small flowers

Rose: basket triangles and squares with square design

Blue: single French knots in centers of squares in basket triangles and squares, inner row of stitching on large flowers, lines in large flower center and in flower petals

Light teal: lines in large flower petals

Aqua: outer row of stitching in large flowers

Dark green: leaves, first side

Sage green: leaves, other side

Olive green: leaf centers

Dark pink: some small flowers

Rose: some small flowers

Black: stems, leaf centers, single French knots in centers of large flowers

Block 4

Dark green: basket handle, around all blocks, solid stripes in blocks

Dark teal: single French knots in basket handle and triangles

Rose: running stitch for dashed lines in basket

Dark pink: large flower centers

Dark yellow: small flowers, centers of large flowers

Salmon: center of largest flower, French knots on small flowers

Olive green: leaves

Black: leaf veins, stems, X's in centers of large flowers

Block 5

Black: Stitch design using a running stitch and backstitch.

FINISHING THE BLOCKS

1. Fold each polka-dot square in half diagonally and press. Center the base of the design on the pressed diagonal line and trace. Embroider all the lines in black, using a running stitch and backstitch.

2. Place Template A on top of the design, aligning the dashed line on the diagonal side of the template with the fold line on the block.

Cut out the triangle shape. Repeat to trim all the embroidered polka-dot squares.

3. Turn all the blocks facedown; lightly spray with starch and press each block. Make sure to protect your ironing board from any additional wax transfer with a pressing cloth.

4. Trim Block 5 (center) to 4½˝ × 4½˝. Trim Blocks 1–4 to 6½˝ × 6½˝.

BLOCK ASSEMBLY

All seam allowances are ¼˝.

1. Pin and then stitch an embroidered Template A triangle to a matching-color floral print Template A triangle. Press. Repeat to make a total of 4 embroidered corner blocks (Figure 1).

2. Stitch a small floral print triangle to the top and bottom of Block 5, centering the triangles on the square. Press toward the triangles (Figure 2). Sew the remaining 2 triangles to the other 2 sides of the block. Press.

3. Trim the block to 6½˝ × 6½˝, centering the white square on point. The 4 corners of the embroidered block will not touch the seamline and will appear to float (Figure 3).

QUILT CENTER ASSEMBLY

1. Lay out all the embroidered and pieced blocks (Figure 4).

2. Stitch the blocks together in rows and press.

3. Stitch the rows together, matching the seams, and press.

Figure 1—make 4.

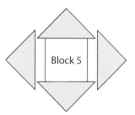

Figure 2

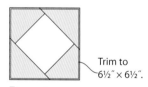

Trim to 6½˝ × 6½˝.

Figure 3

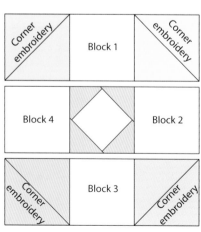

Figure 4

BORDER ASSEMBLY

1. Stitch a light 2½˝ × 15˝ border strip to a black 1½˝ × 15˝ border strip lengthwise. Press toward the black fabric. Repeat with the remaining border strips to make a total of 8 border strip units.

2. Cut the right-hand ends of 4 border strip units at a 45° angle as shown. Cut the left-hand ends of the 4 remaining border strip units at a 45° angle as shown (Figure 5).

Figure 5

3. Stitch the short side of a medium floral print triangle (cut from a 5⅜˝ square) to the angled right-hand end of a border strip unit. Align the pieces at the bottom (black print), offsetting them by ¼˝ for a perfect point. Press.

4. Stitch a left-side cut border strip unit to the other short side of the triangle and press. Trim the top of the triangle even with the light side of the border strip (Figure 6).

Figure 6

5. Repeat Steps 3 and 4 to make 3 additional inner border strips.

6. Refer to Mitered Corner Borders (page 85) to add the inner borders and miter the corners. Trim the excess borders.

7. Fold a 2˝ × 2˝ black square in half diagonally and finger-press. Place on top of a 2˝ × 3½˝ piece as shown (Figure 7), right sides together, and stitch on the diagonal line.

8. Trim to a ¼˝ seam allowance, flip open, and press.

9. Repeat Steps 7 and 8 using the same color of 2˝ × 3½˝ pieces, but making a mirror-image unit.

10. Stitch 2 matching mirror-image units together to make an outer border unit. Press.

11. Repeat Steps 7–10 to make a total of 32 outer border units (Figure 7).

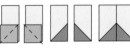

Figure 7

12. Stitch 8 border units together. Press. Repeat to make a second outer border.

13. Stitch the 8-unit outer border strips to the top and bottom of the quilt. Press.

14. Stitch a black triangle to a same-size floral triangle (cut from a 3⅞˝ square) to make a border corner unit. Press. Repeat to make a total of 4 border corner units.

15. Stitch 8 border units together and then stitch a border corner unit to each end. Press. Repeat to make a second long border.

16. Stitch the border strips from the previous step to the left and right sides of the quilt, matching the seams, and press (Figure 8).

Figure 8

FINISHING

1. Layer the quilt top with batting and backing, and quilt as desired.

2. To make the yo-yos, thread a hand-sewing needle and knot an end, leaving a tail after the knot. Insert the needle in the edge of the fabric on the wrong side so the knot will be inside the yo-yo. Working with the wrong side of the fabric toward you, gently turn under approximately ⅛˝ to ¼˝ of the edge of the circle. Sew a running stitch around the edge of the circle, turning the edge as you sew and stopping when you reach where you started. Gently pull the stitching thread until the edges gather to the center. Make a couple of stitches to secure the gathers, and then knot and trim the thread. Finger-press the yo-yo flat with the "hole" in the center.

3. Stitch 4 small yo-yos to the ends of the embroidered stems in the center block, and a large and 2 small yo-yos to the ends of the embroidered stems in each corner block.

4. Stitch a button in the center of each yo-yo.

5. Refer to Binding Basics (page 135) to make the binding and bind the quilt.

MITERED CORNER BORDERS

Measure the length of the quilt top through the center.

Place pins at the centers of both side inner borders and all 4 sides of the quilt top. From the center pin, measure in both directions and mark half the measured length of the quilt top on both side inner borders. Pin the borders to the quilt top, matching the centers and the marked length of the side borders. Stitch the strips to the sides of the quilt top by starting ¼″ in from the beginning edge of the quilt top, backstitching, and then continuing down the length of the side border. Stop stitching ¼″ before the ending edge of the quilt top, at the seam allowance line, and backstitch. The excess length of the side borders will extend beyond each edge. Press the seams toward the borders.

To attach the inner borders to the top and bottom of the quilt center, measure the quilt again horizontally through the center. From the center of each inner border strip, measure in both directions and mark half the measured width of the quilt top. Pin the borders to the quilt, and again start and stop stitching at the previous stitching lines, ¼″ from the quilt edges, and backstitch. The border strips will extend beyond the ends of the quilt. Press the seams toward the borders.

To create the miter, lay the corner on the ironing board. Working with the quilt right side up, lay a border strip on top of the adjacent border.

With right sides up, fold the top border strip under itself so that it meets the edge of the adjacent border and forms a 45° angle. Pin the fold in place.

Position a 90°-angle triangle or ruler over the corner to check that the corner is flat and square. When everything is in place, press the fold firmly.

Remove the pins. Fold the center section of the top diagonally from the corner, right sides together, and align the long edges of the border strips. On the wrong side, place pins near the pressed fold in the corner to secure the border strips.

Beginning at the inside corner at the border seamline, stitch, backstitch, and then stitch along the fold toward the outside point of the border corner, being careful not to allow any stretching to occur. Backstitch at the end. Trim the excess border fabric to a ¼″ seam allowance. Press the seam open.

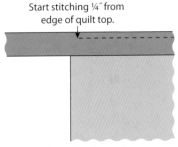

Start stitching ¼″ from edge of quilt top.

Stop stitching ¼″ from edge.

Border strip on top of adjacent strip

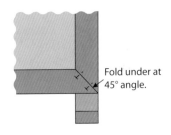

Fold under at 45° angle.

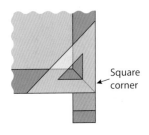

Square corner

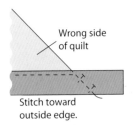

Wrong side of quilt

Stitch toward outside edge.

Stitch mitered corner.

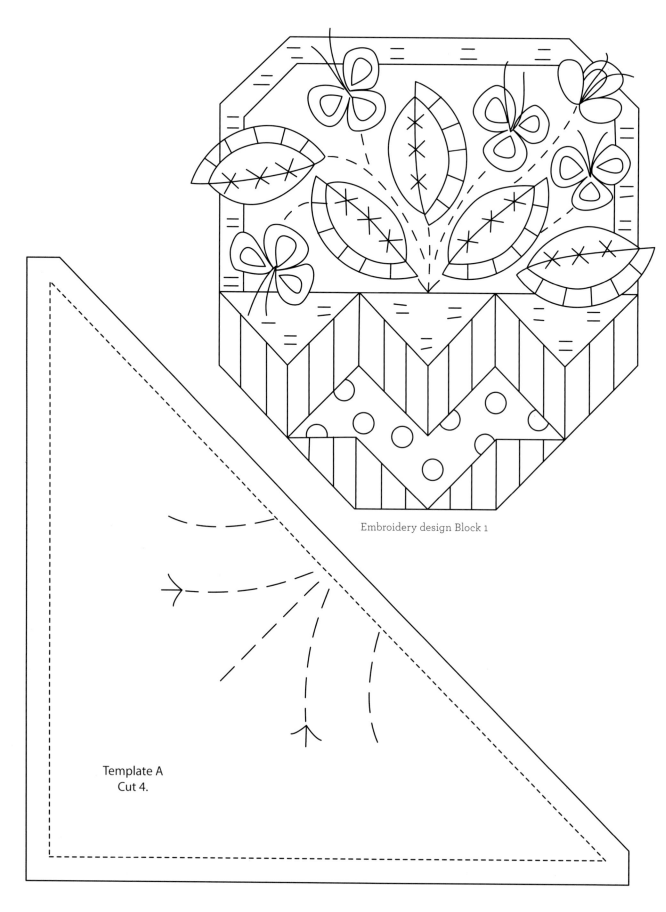

Embroidery design Block 1

Template A
Cut 4.

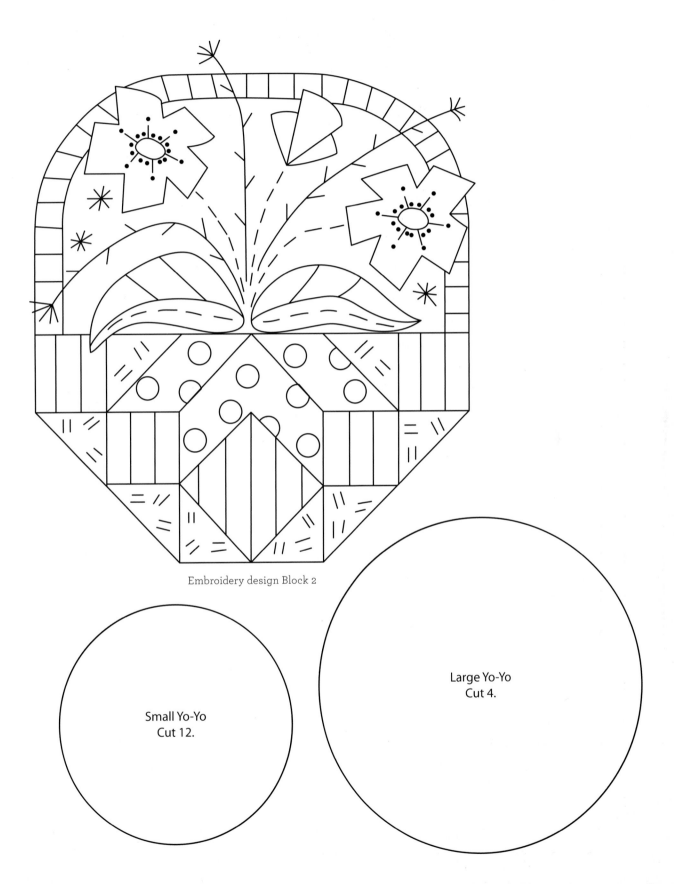

Embroidery design Block 2

Small Yo-Yo
Cut 12.

Large Yo-Yo
Cut 4.

Embroidery design Block 3

Embroidery design Block 4

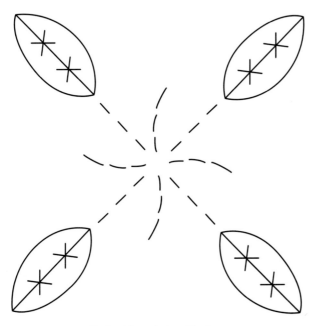

Embroidery design Block 5

Flourishing
Flowers
Pouch

W*hether you fill this elegant little pouch with jewelry, makeup, coupons, notes, or whatever, it's sure to be a handy item for your purse or bag. Make several—keep some and give some as gifts. Just perfect. All the fabrics used in the photographed project are from Lecien.*

by Yoko Saito of Quilt Party

Finished size: 6¾˝ × 4˝

Materials and Supplies

- 1 fat eighth (9˝ × 20˝) of fabric for pouch flap/back
- 1 fat eighth of fabric for pocket
- 1 fat quarter (18˝ × 20˝) of fabric for lining
- 1 fat quarter of fabric for bias binding (or 1 continuous bias strip 1⅜˝ × 35˝)

- 10˝ × 20˝ piece of batting
- 2 buttons, ⅝˝ to ¾˝ in diameter
- 6˝ length of thin elastic for button loops
- Embroidery floss:
    Dark taupe (COSMO #369)
    Dark sage green (COSMO #925)

Brown (COSMO #426)

Dark gray (COSMO #155)

Medium moss green (COSMO #684)

Cream (COSMO #364)

White (COSMO #100)

Cutting

POUCH FLAP/BACK FABRIC

1 from template (page 95)

POCKET FABRIC

1 from template (page 95)

LINING FABRIC

8½˝ × 10˝ for pouch

5½˝ × 8½˝ for pocket

BIAS BINDING FABRIC

2 diagonal strips 1⅜˝ wide and to equal at least 35˝ in length when pieced together

BATTING

9˝ × 11˝ for pouch

5˝ × 9˝ for pocket

ELASTIC CORD

2 lengths 2½˝ for button loops

Embroidery Stitches

French knot   133

Stem stitch   134

Straight stitch   134

Instructions

All seam allowances are ¼˝. Template patterns and embroidery designs can be found on page 95.

EMBROIDERY

1. Transfer the designs onto the pouch flap/back piece (see Transferring the Printed Patterns, page 130).

2. Embroider the design.

Dark taupe:
Stem stitch the radiating flower stems.

Dark sage green:
Stem stitch 2 petals on each stem.

Brown:
Stem stitch a center petal on each stem.

Dark gray:
Stem stitch the hearts in the centers of the large motifs.

Medium moss green:
Add French knots in the centers of the large motifs.

Cream:
Add stem stitches between the petals on the large motifs; then add French knots to the tips of the short spokes.

Stem stitch the short center spokes of the small motifs; then add French knots to the tips.

White:
Use stem stitches for the tips of the long spokes on the small motifs.

CONSTRUCTION

1. Layer the embroidered pouch piece, right side down; batting; and lining, right side up. Baste the layers together and quilt as desired.

2. Trim using pouch template pattern on page 95 (Figure 1).

3. Layer the pocket and pocket lining right sides together on top of the batting. Pin the layers together and stitch along a long edge. Trim the batting away within the seam allowance to reduce bulk.

4. Fold the pocket fabric over the batting at the seam so both fabrics are right side out. Baste the layers together and quilt as desired.

5. Trace the lower half of the pouch template pattern on page 95 onto the quilted pocket and trim (Figure 2).

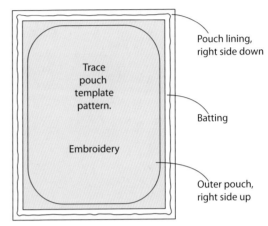

Pouch lining, right side down

Batting

Outer pouch, right side up

Trace pouch template pattern.

Embroidery

Figure 1

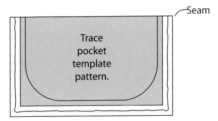

Seam

Trace pocket template pattern.

Figure 2

ASSEMBLY

1. Use the pouch template to mark the button loop positions on the lining side of the embroidered end of the pouch. The loops should be 3˝ apart.

2. Fold a 2½˝ elastic length in half and pin it in place on the lining side, matching up the ends with the raw edges of the flap. Baste the elastic loop in place. Repeat to make the second loop (Figure 3).

3. To assemble the pouch, align the curved edges of the pocket, right side up, with the curved edges of the pouch, lining side up, at the end without button loops. Pin the pocket in place (Figure 3).

4. Sew in place around the outside edge of the pocket (Figure 3).

5. Fold and press a long edge of the bias binding strip over ¼˝ to the wrong side. To finish the raw edges of the pouch, pin the bias binding all around the embroidered side of the pouch, aligning the raw edges. Finish the binding ends nicely as described in Finishing the Binding Ends (page 136). Stitch in place around the entire pouch. Fold the binding over the raw edges and hand stitch the folded edge of the binding to the front side of the pouch.

6. To make the button loops lie in the right direction, pin them against the bias binding, sticking out past the edge of the pouch, and stitch in place by hand (Figure 4).

7. Fold the flap closed and mark the centers of the button loops on the pocket front. Stitch the buttons in place as marked (Figure 5).

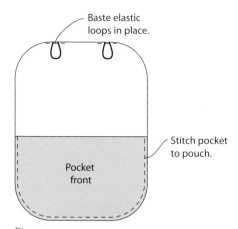

Baste elastic loops in place.

Stitch pocket to pouch.

Pocket front

Figure 3

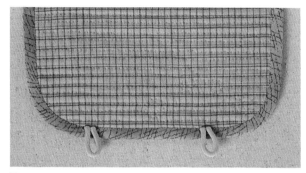

Figure 4

Figure 5

Flourishing Flowers Pouch

Cut 2 of fabric for pouch and lining.
Cut 1 of batting for pouch.

Cut 2 of fabric for pocket and pocket lining.
Cut 1 of batting for pocket.

For pocket, trace and cut only to this line.

Loop   Loop

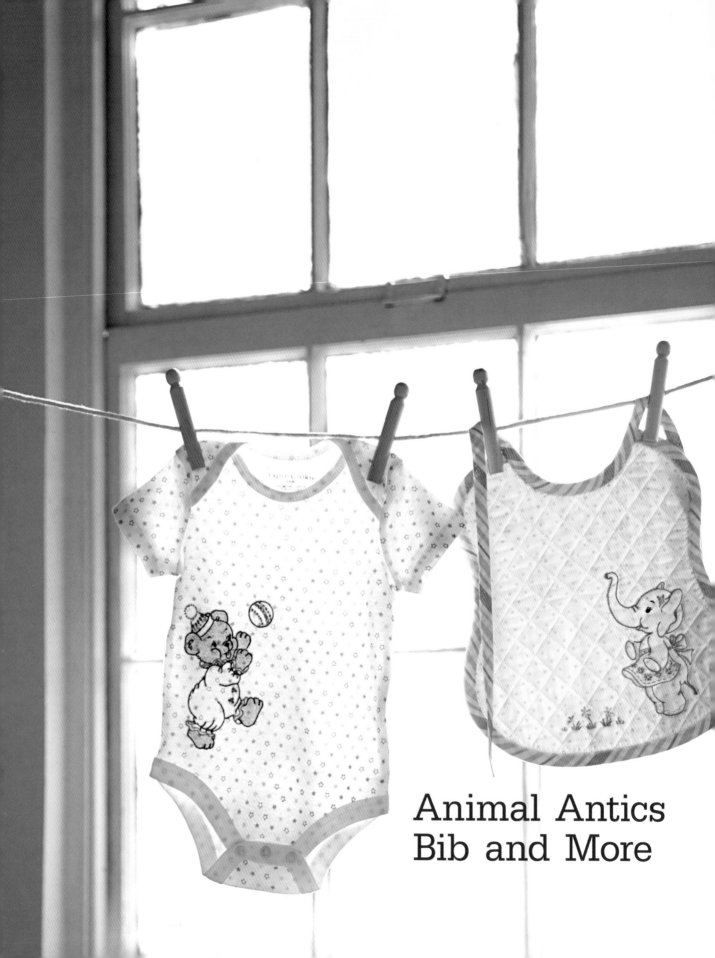

Animal Antics
Bib and More

These fun elephant and baby bear designs add the cuteness factor to this bib. They can also bring a colorful bit of amusement to blankets, T-shirts, pant legs, Onesies, or anything else you can think of. Be creative! The fabrics used in the sample are Lecien Color Basic Medium Dots in white with pink dots and Stripes in pink.

by Loyce Saxton
of Yesterday's Charm

Finished size:
bib, 10½˝ × 12˝;
bear motif, 3½˝ × 6˝;
elephant motif, 6˝ × 5½˝

Materials and Supplies

- 12˝ × 13˝ piece of light print or solid fabric for bib front

- 12˝ × 13˝ piece of coordinating fabric for bib back

- Embroidery floss:

  For the elephant:
  Gray (COSMO #892)
  White (COSMO #2500)
  Black (COSMO #600)
  Pink (COSMO #203)
  Blue (COSMO #372)
  Green (COSMO #272)
  Yellow (COSMO #700)

  For the bear:
  Brown (COSMO #311)
  Black (COSMO #600)
  Blue (COSMO #2214)
  Red (COSMO #345)
  Green (COSMO #324)
  Orange (COSMO #2402)

- 2 bias strips 2˝ × 36˝ of striped fabric or 2 pieces 36˝ long of extra-wide double-fold bias tape for binding

- 12˝ × 13˝ piece of batting

- Crayola crayon in raw umber for the bear

Embroidery Stitches

French knot   133

Lazy daisy stitch   133

Running stitch   133

Satin stitch   133

Stem stitch   134

Straight stitch   134

EMBELLISHING READY-MADE ITEMS

- Onesie, T-shirt, pants, overalls, bag, burp cloth, blanket, and such

- Freezer paper

- Fabric stabilizer for knit garments, such as Shape-Flex (by C&T Publishing) or other lightweight fusible interfacing

Instructions

Template patterns can be found on page 138. Prewash ready-made garments without fabric softener to remove sizing if you plan to use crayons.

EMBELLISHING READY-MADES

1. Cut freezer paper 1˝ larger all around than the embroidery design. Iron the freezer paper, shiny side down, to the wrong side of the garment to hold the fabric in place while you are tracing. Transfer the design onto the item (see Transferring the Printed Patterns, page 130).

TIP

If the item is stretchy, use a fabric stabilizer to make stitching easier. Embroidering without a hoop allows you to get into small areas and prevents the fabric from being stretched out of shape.

2. Color and/or embroider the design, referring to Embroidery (at right and next page).

EMBROIDERY

Use 2 strands of floss and stem stitch for all embroidery, unless otherwise noted. Embroidery designs are on page 101.

1. Transfer the bib outline and embroidery design onto the bib front fabric (see Transferring the Printed Patterns, page 130).

2. Embroider the design, referring to the detail photos (page 99) for additional floss placement details.

3. When the embroidery is finished, press face-down on a terry-cloth towel.

For the Elephant

Gray:
Stitch around the elephant.

White:
Add the toenails.

Black:
Satin stitch the eye and add stem stitches for the lashes and brow.

Pink:
Stitch the apron outline and add running stitch for the inner-edge line.

Stitch the pink flower petals in lazy daisy stitch and add a French knot for the flower center.

Blue:
Stitch flowers in lazy daisy stitch on the apron, head, and ground.

Green:
Stitch the grass and use straight stitches on the apron flowers.

Add leaves in lazy daisy stitch for the flower on the head.

Yellow:
Stitch the yellow flower in lazy daisy stitch and add French knots for flower centers.

For the Bear

Color the bear's head, ears, and paws with a regular crayon. To heat set the crayon and remove excess wax, place the piece, crayon side down, on several layers of clean white paper towels and iron on the cotton setting from the back side for about 30 seconds; then remove the freezer paper.

Brown:
Stitch the outline of the bear's head, ears, and paws.

Black:
Satin stitch the center of the eyes and the nose, and stem stitch the rest of the eye, lashes, and brow.

Blue:
Stitch the outfit and the outline of the hat, and straight stitch a side of the cross-stitches on the ball.

Red:
Stitch the tongue, use lazy daisy stitches on the hat, and add French knots for the buttons and on the ball.

Green:
Stitch the outfit trim, straight stitch the other side of the cross-stitches on the ball, and add French knots on the hat.

Orange:
Add French knots for the buttons, on the hat, and on the ball.

BIB ASSEMBLY

1. Tape together the top and bottom halves of the bib template pattern along the join line and trace on the embroidered fabric. Layer the backing fabric, right side down; batting; and embroidered bib fabric, right side up. Pin or baste all 3 layers together (Figure 1).

2. Quilt around the embroidery design and stipple or crosshatch quilt the background. Cut out the bib on the traced line.

3. Fold the binding strips in half lengthwise, right side out, and press (Figure 2). Fold an edge in toward the center crease and press again (Figure 3).

4. Line up the remaining unfolded edge of a binding strip with the raw edge of the bib as shown and sew in place all around the bib body, using a ⅜″ seam (Figure 4). Leave the neck opening for later (Figure 5).

5. Wrap the folded side of the binding around to the back and sew by hand or machine (decorative machine stitches would look nice).

6. Measure 14″ from an end of the remaining binding strip (for a tie) and then begin sewing to the neckline as in Step 4. Wrap the binding to the back and stitch down as in Step 5 (Figure 6).

7. For the ties, fold both edges under evenly. Topstitch closed by machine, or hand sew invisibly.

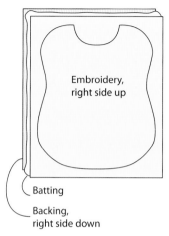

Embroidery, right side up

Batting

Backing, right side down

Figure 1

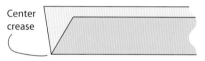

Center crease

Figure 2

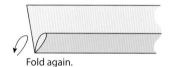

Fold again.

Figure 3

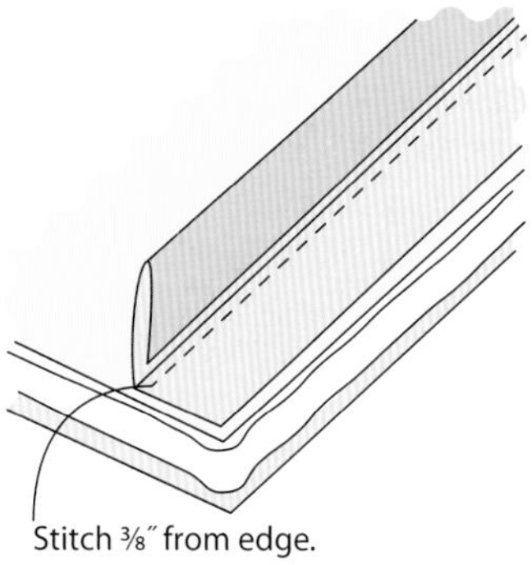

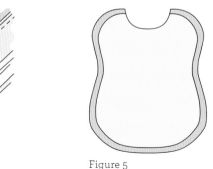

Stitch ⅜″ from edge.

Figure 4

Figure 5

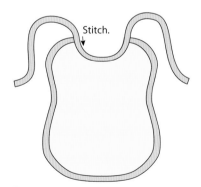

Stitch.

Figure 6

Blooming Season Pillow

S pring is my favorite time of year! The birds are singing, the blossoms are blooming, and everything is sunny and bright. When I sat down to draw a design for this project, I wanted it to reflect my joy of spring with a nod to appliqué quilt wreaths. I used Crackle Wheat fabric from Moda.

by Kathy Schmitz

Finished size: 12″ × 12″

Materials and Supplies

- 1 square 10″ × 10″ of fabric for embroidery background

- 4 pieces 3½″ × 7″ of blue striped fabric for pillow front (Change the orientation of the cuts as needed to get the stripes running parallel to the short sides.)

- 4 squares 3½″ × 3½″ of light print fabric for pillow front

- 1 square 13″ × 13″ of fabric for pillow back

- Embroidery floss:
  Variegated blue
  (COSMO Seasons #8025)

- Fiberfill

Embroidery Stitches

Buttonhole stitch   132

French knot   133

Lazy daisy stitch   133

Running stitch   133

Satin stitch   133

Stem stitch   134

Instructions

The embroidery design can be found on the next page. All embroidery uses 2 strands of floss. All seam allowances are ¼˝.

EMBROIDERY

1. Transfer the design onto the fabric (see Transferring the Printed Patterns, page 130).

TIP

When working a design in a single colorway of variegated floss, consider how the color changes as you embroider different sections of the design.

2. Embroider the design.

First, stem stitch all the solid lines.

Then complete all the different types of stitches in a small area before moving on to another section.

Add French knots for all the dots.

Satin stitch the bees' stripes.

Use lazy daisy stitches for the leaf details and the small bloom petals.

Buttonhole stitch the circles in the center of the stars and the base of the petals on the small blooms.

Use running stitches in the leaves of the large flowers.

PILLOW ASSEMBLY

1. Press the embroidered piece well and trim to 7˝ × 7˝, with the design centered.

2. Sew 3½˝ × 7˝ blue striped pieces to 2 opposite sides of the embroidered piece. Press.

Embroidery

3. Sew a 3½˝ × 3½˝ light print square to each end of the remaining 3½˝ × 7˝ blue striped pieces. Press.

Make 2.

4. Sew the pieced border strips to the top and bottom of the embroidered piece. Press.

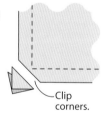

Completed pillow front

5. Pin the pillow front and the 13˝ × 13˝ backing square right sides together and sew around all 4 sides of the pillow, leaving a 3˝ opening at the bottom for turning and stuffing.

6. Clip the corners and turn the pillow right side out.

7. Stuff with fiberfill.

8. Hand stitch the opening closed.

Clip corners.

Lovely Letter
Carrier

This letter carrier will look pretty just about anywhere you can think to hang it ... with pockets for correspondence, stamps, and pens or letter openers. Organizers like this are functional and pretty!

by Amy Sinibaldi of nanaCompany

Finished size: 12½″ × 9½″

Materials and Supplies

- 1 fat quarter (18″ × 22″) of blue-and-white ticking stripe fabric for pockets

- 1 fat quarter (18″ × 22″) of white floral fabric for background

- 1 fat quarter (18″ × 22″) of backing fabric

- 1 scrap at least 7″ × 7″ of solid pink fabric for embroidered patch

- 1 scrap at least 2″ × 4″ of multicolored floral fabric for lower pocket binding

- 2 scraps at least 2″ × 2″ of 2 different fabrics for "stamps"

- ¼ yard of light green floral fabric for binding

- ½ yard of batting, at least 20″ wide

- ½ yard of ½″-wide crochet trim, lace, or rickrack

- Embroidery floss:
    Gray (COSMO #155)
    Light blue (COSMO #980)
    Olive green (COSMO #675)
    Sage green (COSMO #923)
    Pink (COSMO #104)
    Dark pink (COSMO #106)
    Ivory (COSMO #140)
    Mustard yellow (COSMO #574)

- 4″ × 4″ square of paper-backed fusible web

- 1 button

- 2 grommets, approximately ½″ in diameter

- ½ yard of ribbon or twine for hanging

Embroidery Stitches

Backstitch   132

French knot   133

Lazy daisy stitch   133

Running stitch   133

Satin stitch   133

Stem stitch   134

Cutting

SOLID PINK FABRIC

1 piece 4½″ × 5½″ for embroidery background

TICKING STRIPE FABRIC

1 piece 6½″ × 9½″ for large pocket

1 piece 3½″ × 6½″ for medium pocket

1 piece 3″ × 3½″ for small lower pocket

WHITE FLORAL FABRIC

1 piece 9½″ × 12½″ for base

BACKING FABRIC

1 piece 6½″ × 12½″ for pocket

1 piece 9½″ × 12½″ for base

MULTICOLORED FLORAL FABRIC

1 piece 1½″ × 3½″ for small pocket binding

LIGHT GREEN FLORAL FABRIC

2 strips 2½″ × WOF* for binding

CROCHET TRIM

1 piece 3½″ long

1 piece 12½″ long

BATTING

1 piece 4″ × 5″ for embroidered patch

1 piece 6½″ × 9½″ for pocket

1 piece 9½″ × 12½″ for base

WOF = width of fabric

Instructions

The embroidery design is on the previous page. All seam allowances are ¼".

EMBROIDERY

1. Transfer the design onto the pink fabric (see Transferring the Printed Patterns, page 130).

2. Place the 4" × 5" piece of batting behind the pink fabric, so that later when you hand appliqué the patch onto the front pocket you're simply folding the fabric behind the batting.

3. Embroider the design through both layers, referring to the photo (below) for color placement.

Gray:
Outline *Letters* in backstitch using 3 strands of floss.

Stitch lazy daisy flowers using 2 strands of floss.

Light blue:
Satin stitch *Letters* using 2 strands of floss.

Stitch lazy daisy flowers using 2 strands of floss.

Olive green:
Stem stitch the vine lines using 2 strands of floss.

Backstitch the leaves using 2 strands of floss.

Sage green:
Backstitch a line through the center of each leaf using 1 strand of floss.

Stitch French knots using 3 strands of floss.

Pink:
Stitch French knots using 3 strands of floss.

Dark pink:
Stitch lazy daisy flowers using 2 strands of floss.

Stitch French knots using 3 strands of floss.

Ivory:
Stitch French knots using 3 strands of floss.

Mustard yellow:
Stitch French knots using 3 strands of floss.

FRONT POCKET ASSEMBLY

1. Sew the 3½˝ length of crochet trim approximately ⅛˝ from a 3½˝ edge of the 3˝ × 3½˝ lower pocket piece. The trimmed edge is now the top of this pocket.

2. Refer to Binding Basics (page 135) to make and attach the white floral binding to the top edge of this pocket piece.

3. Following the manufacturer's instructions, iron paper-backed fusible web to the wrong side of the 2 fabric scraps for "stamps." Cut out a piece 1˝ × 1¼˝ from the first fabric and a piece 1¼˝ × 1½˝ from the other.

4. Fuse the larger "stamp" patch into place on the lower pocket, approximately ¾˝ in from the upper right-hand corner. Fuse the smaller "stamp" patch centered on top of the larger patch.

5. Zigzag stitch by machine around the outside of both stamp patches. By hand, backstitch "25¢" and sew a running stitch around the inner stamp patch using dark blue embroidery floss, as shown (below).

6. Place the completed lower pocket, right side up, on top of the 3½˝ × 6½˝ medium pocket piece, right side up, aligning the bottom edges. Stitch together around the left, bottom, and right sides, ⅛˝ from the raw edges.

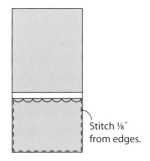

Stitch ⅛˝ from edges.

7. Sew the double pocket from Step 6 to the right-hand side of the 6½˝ × 9½˝ large pocket piece, right sides together. Iron flat.

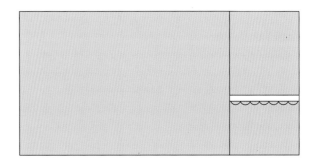

8. Hand appliqué the embroidered *Letters* patch to the center of the large pocket. Using the light pink floss, sew a running stich around the patch through the pocket fabric.

9. Layer the 6½˝ × 12½˝ piece of backing fabric, right side down; batting; and assembled pocket, right side up. Pin all 3 layers together.

10. Using the sage green floss, sew a running stitch along the seam joining the pockets.

11. Sew the 12½˝ length of crochet trim at the top edge of the pocket, approximately ⅛˝ below the raw edge.

12. Refer again to Binding Basics (page 135) to make and attach the green floral binding along this top edge. Trim the binding even with the sides.

13. Referring to the finished project photo (below), hand sew the button to the top center of the upper right pocket.

BASE ASSEMBLY

1. Layer the 9½˝ × 12½˝ piece of backing fabric, right side down; batting; and 9½˝ × 12½˝ piece of white floral fabric, right side up. Baste all 3 layers together.

2. Quilt as desired.

3. Place the pocket on top of the base, aligning at the bottom edge. Sew along the left, bottom, and right sides of the pocket to attach it to the base, approximately ⅛˝ from the raw edges.

4. Topstitch along the vertical seam on the pocket. This divides the single large front pocket into 2 smaller pockets.

5. Attach the remaining green binding all around the outer raw edge of the base. Refer to Finishing the Binding Ends (page 136) to join the ends. Hand sew the binding on the back side of the letter carrier.

6. Attach grommets to the top edge. They should be placed about 2˝ from the sides and about ¾˝ below the top edge.

7. Using ribbon or twine, tie the letter carrier to a coat hanger, a chair, or anywhere you'd like!

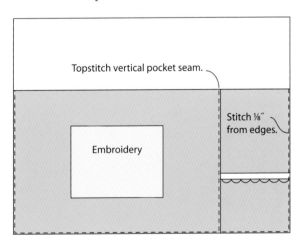

Topstitch vertical pocket seam.

Stitch ⅛˝ from edges.

Embroidery

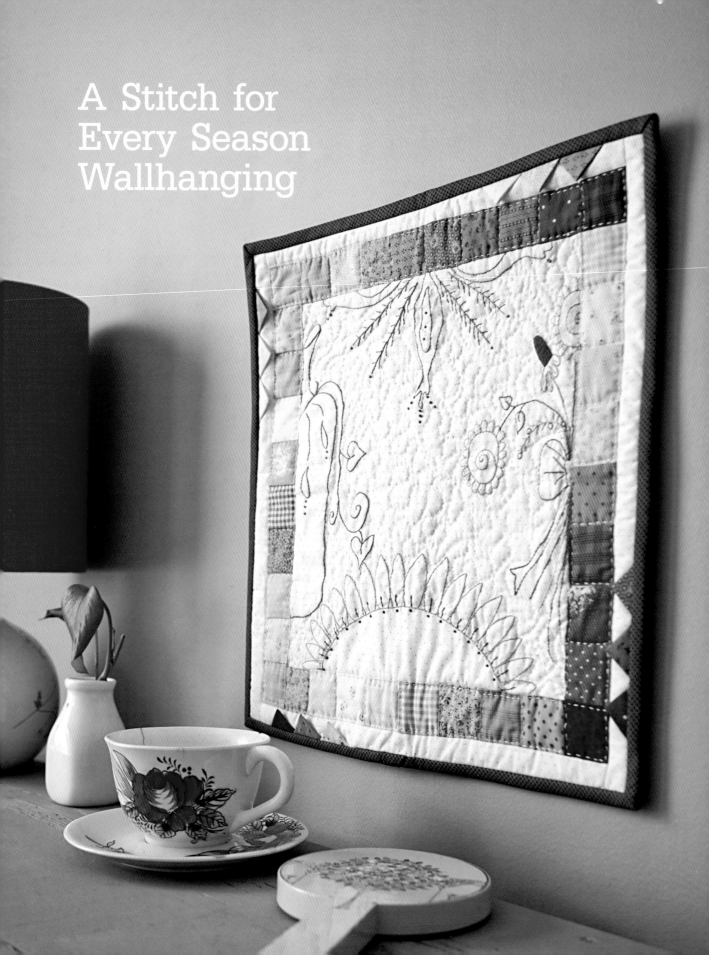

A Stitch for
Every Season
Wallhanging

These four seasonal designs come together to create a wallhanging to use all year long. The wonderful colors and simple stitches make this a perfect addition to any decor. I used a variety of Lecien fabric prints and the Quilters Basic collection.

by Tracy Souza
of Plumcute Designs

Finished size: 16˝ × 16˝

Materials and Supplies

- 1 fat quarter (18˝ × 22˝) of white fabric with green polka dots

- Scraps of various prints in pink, red, orange, yellow, green, blue, purple/gray, and charcoal

- Embroidery floss:

    Dark green (COSMO #119)

    Orange (COSMO #129)

    Brown (COSMO #386)

    Gray (COSMO #475)

    Light green (COSMO #631)

    Yellow (COSMO #703)

    Pink (COSMO #854)

    Light pink (COSMO #852)

    Red (COSMO #857)

    Cream (COSMO #364)

- 1 fat quarter (18˝ × 22˝) of fabric for backing

- 18˝ × 18˝ piece of batting

- 2 yards of purchased double-fold binding

Embroidery Stitches

Backstitch   132

French knot   133

Satin stitch   133

Cutting

WHITE FABRIC

1 square 12½˝ × 12½˝

2 strips 1¼˝ × 15½˝

2 strips 1¼˝ × 17˝

PRINT SCRAPS

7 squares 2˝ × 2˝ of pink

5 squares 2˝ × 2˝ of red

4 squares 2˝ × 2˝ of orange

7 squares 2˝ × 2˝ of yellow

6 squares 2˝ × 2˝ of green

11 squares 2˝ × 2˝ of blue

5 squares 2˝ × 2˝ of purple/gray

3 squares 2˝ × 2˝ of charcoal

BACKING FABRIC

1 square 18˝ × 18˝

Instructions

WALLHANGING CONSTRUCTION

All seam allowances are ¼˝.

1. Arranging squares of the same color by value from light to dark, piece the 2˝ × 2˝ squares into 4 rows as follows:

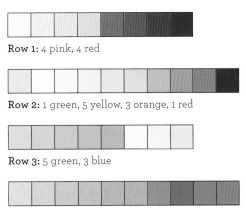

Row 1: 4 pink, 4 red

Row 2: 1 green, 5 yellow, 3 orange, 1 red

Row 3: 5 green, 3 blue

Row 4: 5 blue, 3 purple/gray, 2 charcoal

The remaining 2˝ × 2˝ squares will be used later to make prairie points.

2. Press all the seams in the same direction.

3. Sew the rows onto the white background square, following the assembly diagram.

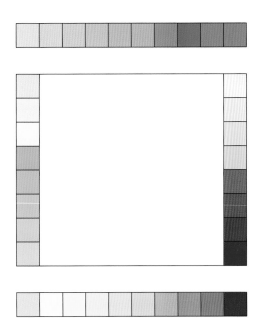

4. Press the seams away from the center square.

5. Sew the 1¼˝ × 15½˝ white strips to the top and bottom of the quilt top; press the seams toward the pieced border.

6. Sew the white 1¼˝ × 17˝ strips to the remaining 2 sides; press the seams toward the pieced border.

EMBROIDERY

All embroidery uses 2 strands of floss. Embroidery designs can be found on pages 116 and 117.

1. Transfer the designs onto the white center square of the quilt top (see Transferring the Printed Patterns, page 130). Center the Winter Snowflake along the blue/purple/gray border strip, and the Summer Sunflower along the green/yellow/orange border strip. Place the Spring Bouquet roughly centered along the pink/red border strip, making sure not to overlap the other motifs. Place the Fall Pumpkin roughly centered along the blue/green border strip, again making sure not to overlap the other motifs.

2. Embroider the design.

Winter Snowflake:
Stitch French knots and backstitch the rest of the design using gray floss.

Spring Bouquet:
Backstitch all the flower stems and leaves using dark green floss.

Backstitch the pine bough using light green floss and the berries using orange floss.

Backstitch the swirl flower centers using pink floss and the petals using light pink floss.

Satin stitch the coneflower center using brown floss.

Backstitch the coneflower petals and add a long straight stitch down the center of each petal using yellow floss.

Backstitch the bow using red floss.

Summer Sunflower:
Backstitch the center of each petal and stitch French knots at the base of each petal using brown floss.

Backstitch the rest of the design using yellow floss.

Fall Pumpkin:
Sew French knots and backstitch the outline and details of the pumpkin using orange floss.

Backstitch the pumpkin stem using brown floss.

Backstitch the vines and leaves using dark green floss.

3. Press the quilt top.

FINISHING

Sandwich the backing, batting, and embroidered quilt top. Baste and quilt as desired. I hand quilted using 2 strands of cream-colored floss.

Prairie Points

1. Fold and press a remaining 2″ × 2″ square in half diagonally, wrong sides together, to create a triangle.

2. Fold and press the triangle in half again along the long side to complete the prairie point.

3. Repeat Steps 1 and 2 with the remaining 2″ × 2″ squares to make a total of 12 prairie points.

4. Referring to the finished quilt photo (page 112) as a guide, position the prairie points as detailed below, aligning the raw edges of the prairie points with the raw edges of the quilt, and pin in place.

Purple/gray and charcoal along the Spring side

Pinks and red along the Summer side

Yellows and orange along the Fall side

Blues along the Winter side

5. Bind using your preferred method or refer to Binding Basics (page 135) for instructions. Stitching down the binding will also attach the prairie points.

Summer Sunflower

Spring Bouquet

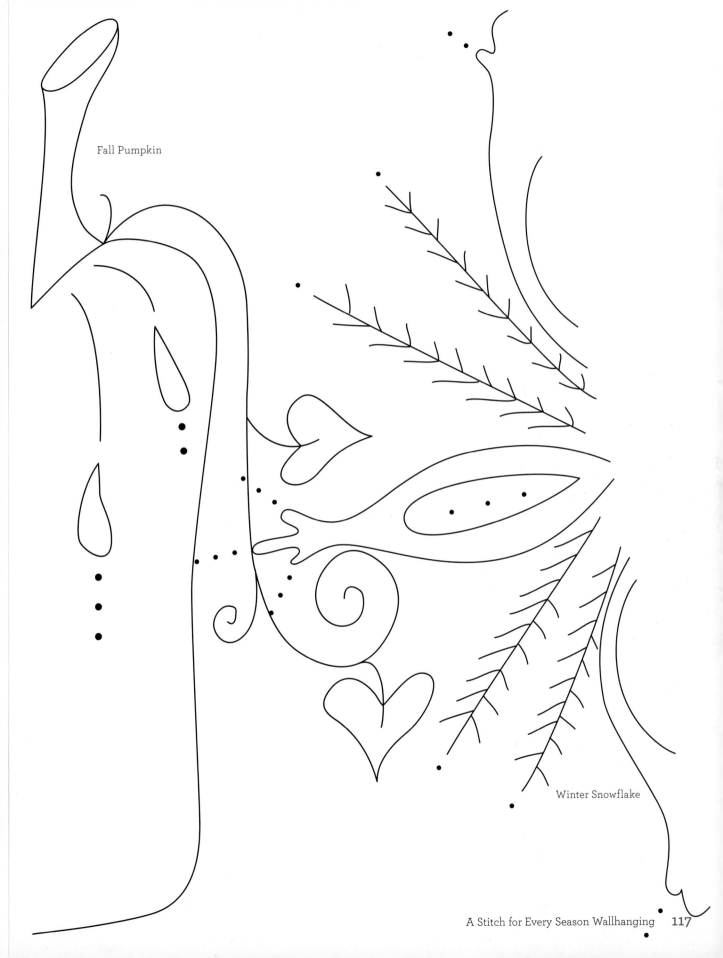

Fall Pumpkin

Winter Snowflake

Instructions

EMBROIDERY

Use 3 strands of floss for all chain and stem stitches. Use 2 strands for all other stitches.

1. Transfer the design onto the linen (see Transferring the Printed Patterns, page 130).

2. Embroider the design.

Brown:
Stem stitch the bunny's head and ears.

Satin stitch the eye and nose.

Use straight stitches for the whiskers.

Backstitch the mouth and paws.

Chain stitch the purse handle.

Coral:
Stem stitch the outlines of the dress.

Backstitch the collar and tie.

Pink:
Stem stitch the cup.

Backstitch the purse.

Use French knots for the flower centers on the purse.

Orange:
Backstitch the flowers on the cup.

Green:
Stitch lazy daisy stitches for the leaves.

Light pink:
Backstitch the inside of the ears.

Light orange:
Stitch lazy daisy flowers on the purse.

Stem stitch the thread.

Gray:
Straight stitch the needle.

CONSTRUCTION

All seam allowances are ¼˝.

1. Trim the embroidered square to 5½˝ × 5½˝.

2. Sew 5 of the 1˝ × 1½˝ assorted-fabric pieces together at the short ends and press. Repeat with the remaining 5 pieces.

3. Sew the pieced borders to the sides of the embroidered square and press toward the borders (Figure 1).

4. Sew the print strips to the top and bottom of the embroidered square and press toward the borders.

5. With right sides together, stitch the pincushion front to the pincushion back, leaving a 2˝ opening at the center bottom and backstitching at the beginning and end.

6. Turn right side out and gently push out the corners. Fill with ground walnut shells. Slipstitch the opening closed.

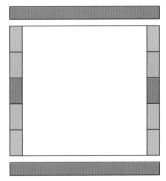

Figure 1

Sparkling
Fox Clutch

*G*rab this sparkly fox clutch for a fun night on the town. The white linen clutch sports an adorable fox that's stitched with sparkly metallic embroidery floss. The clutch is finished with a bright pink wristlet handle. I used a pink dot fabric from my Picnic Pals collection from Clothworks Textiles.

by Alyssa Thomas
of Penguin & Fish

Finished size: 10½″ × 5½″

Materials and Supplies

- 1 fat quarter (18″ × 22″) or ⅓ yard of white linen

- Embroidery floss:
  Yellow metallic (COSMO Sparkles #2)
  Orange metallic (COSMO Sparkles #6)
  Black metallic (COSMO Sparkles #7)

- 1 fat quarter of print fabric for handle and lining

- ⅓ yard of 20″-wide stiff interfacing, such as Timtex (by C&T Publishing)

- 9″-long zipper

- Metal D-ring, ¾″ wide

- Template plastic or thin cardboard

Embroidery Stitches

Backstitch	132
Satin stitch	133
Straight stitch	134

Cutting

Trace the template patterns A, B, C, D, and E (pages 139 and 140) onto template plastic or thin cardboard. Cut out on the drawn lines.

WHITE LINEN

1 square 11″ × 11″ for embroidery

1 of Template A

2 each of Templates B, C, D, and E

2 pieces 1½″ × 4″ for zipper ends

PRINT FABRIC

2 pieces 6″ × 11″ for lining

1 square 3″ × 3″ for D-ring tab

1 piece 3″ × 17″ for handle

STIFF INTERFACING

2 pieces 6″ × 11″

Instructions

All seam allowances are ¼˝.

EMBROIDERY

Use a doubled strand of single-ply Sparkles for all embroidery—no need to separate the plies. The embroidery design is on page 129.

1. Transfer the design onto the fabric (see Transferring the Printed Patterns, page 130).

2. Embroider the design.

Orange:
Fill the ears and tip of the nose with a satin stitch.

Backstitch the outlines on the head and body.

Fill the tail with straight stitches.

Yellow:
Fill the body and face with straight stitches.

Black:
Fill the legs with a satin stitch.

Backstitch the eyes, the snout, and the outline of the front of the body and the tail.

FRONT AND BACK EXTERIOR PIECING

1. Press the embroidered white linen fabric. Avoid pressing the actual embroidery, as it is heat sensitive.

2. Use Template A to trim the embroidery, referring to the finished project photo (page 122) for placement.

3. Place the embroidered A on top of an interfacing piece, aligning the trimmed bottom left corner of A with the bottom left corner of the interfacing.

4. With right sides together, place B on top of A, matching the raw edges.

5. Sew B to A through the stabilizer (Figure 1).

6. Open up B and finger-press it flat. Topstitch B ⅛˝ from the seam.

7. Repeat Steps 4–6 to add C, D, and E.

8. Trim the fabric along the edges of the interfacing to complete the exterior front of the clutch (Figure 2).

9. Repeat Steps 3–8 to make the exterior back of the clutch, using the Template A piece and the remaining B, C, D, and E pieces.

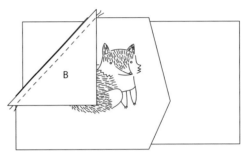

Figure 1

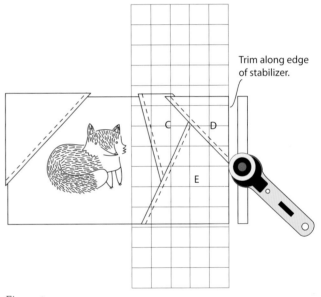

Trim along edge of stabilizer.

Figure 2

ASSEMBLY

1. Fold each of the 2 white linen pieces for the zipper ends in half so the short ends meet. Press.

2. Place the folded edge of the fabric so it overlaps the zipper by ¼˝. Pin the fabric in place and sew along the folded edge with a ⅛˝ seam allowance, making sure not to sew on top of the zipper stop (Figure 3).

3. Open the zipper and repeat Step 2 at the opposite end.

4. Lay out the clutch exterior front, right side up. With right sides together, place the edge of the zipper tape on the top edge of the front exterior piece, centering the zipper across the exterior front (Figure 4).

5. Place a lining piece, right side down, on top of the exterior front/zipper. You should now have the front exterior piece and a lining piece with the zipper sandwiched between them, all with the top edges aligned. Pin the top edge in place.

6. Using a zipper foot, sew along the pinned edge about ⅛˝ away from the zipper (Figure 5).

7. Open the exterior front and the lining so the wrong sides are together and the zipper is visible. Press, avoiding the embroidery (Figure 6).

8. Layer the remaining lining piece, right side up; the assembled front/zipper piece, right side up with the zipper at the top; and the back exterior, wrong side up, all aligned along the top edges, sandwiching the zipper tape in between the back lining and the back exterior. Pin in place along the top.

9. Using a zipper foot, sew along the pinned edge about ⅛˝ away from the zipper (Figure 7).

10. Trim the overhanging edges of the zipper end fabric.

Figure 3

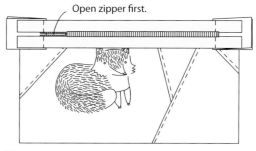

Figure 4

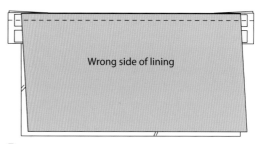

Figure 5

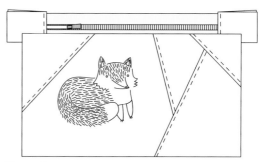

Figure 6

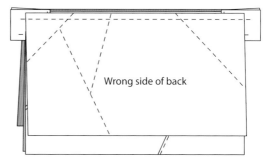

Figure 7

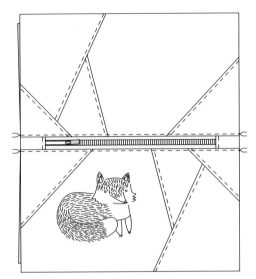

Figure 8

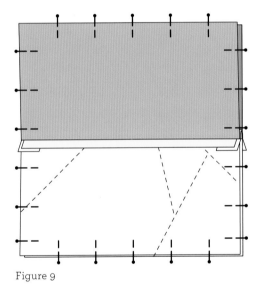

Figure 9

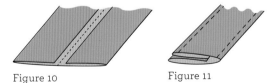

Figure 10   Figure 11

Figure 12

11. Open the back exterior piece and the lining so the wrong sides are together and the zipper is visible. The zipper should be sitting in the middle of the front and back exterior pieces. Press the lining and exteriors away from the zipper teeth (Figure 8).

12. Topstitch along the edge of the folded fabric ⅛″ away from the seam, along both sides of the zipper (Figure 8).

13. *Important:* Make sure the zipper is open.

14. Open the fabric pieces and align them so the right sides of the exterior pieces are facing each other and the right sides of the lining pieces are facing each other.

15. Pin along the entire outside edge. When you get to the middle, where the zipper ends are, fold the zipper ends so that the fold is directed toward the lining pieces (Figure 9). It will be a bit bulky here. Set aside.

16. Fold the 3″ × 3″ fabric square for the D-ring tab in half, with wrong sides together, and press. Unfold and, with wrong sides together, fold an edge to the crease and press. Repeat with the opposite edge (Figure 10). Refold the fabric along the original crease.

17. Topstitch along the folded edges with a ⅛″ seam (Figure 11).

18. Wrap the fabric tab around the flat side of the D-ring and fold the tab in half around the straight edge of the D-ring. Pin the ends together (Figure 12).

19. Place the fabric tab between the exterior pieces of the bag along a short edge, 1½″ from the zipper. The D-ring should be inside the clutch, and the raw edges of the tab will stick out ¼″. Pin the tab in place (Figure 13).

20. Sew around the entire pinned edge, starting 1″ in on the long edge of the lining and ending 1″ in on the other side of the long edge of the lining, leaving an opening to turn the clutch right side out.

21. Clip the corners (Figure 14).

22. Turn the clutch right side out through the opening in the lining and push out all the corners.

23. Fold the lining seam allowances at the opening to the wrong side and hand stitch closed invisibly (Figure 15). Push the lining to the inside of the clutch.

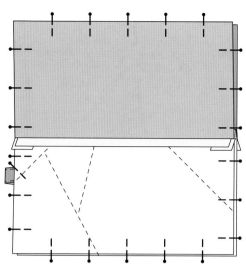

Figure 13

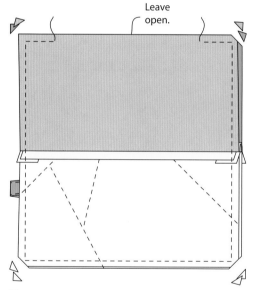

Leave open.

Figure 14

Figure 15

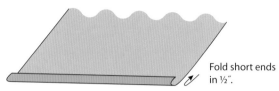
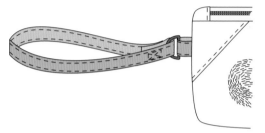

Figure 17

Figure 18

HANDLE

1. Fold the short ends of the handle fabric over ½˝, with wrong sides together, and press (Figure 17).

2. Repeat Assembly, Steps 16 and 17 (page 127), to fold and topstitch the handle strip along its length and along the short ends.

3. Going from the front to the back of the clutch, thread an end of the handle strip through the D-ring about 1½˝. Pin the 1½˝ end to the handle, forming a loop.

4. Place the opposite end of the handle so it overlaps the 1½˝ end by 1˝. Pin to the 1½˝ end.

5. Sew a rectangle through the 3 layers of the handle, securing the handle in place around the D-ring. Sew an X through the rectangle for extra stability (Figure 18).

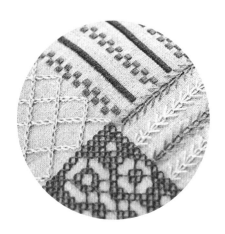

Embroidery

Preparing the Fabric

For most of the projects in this book, the embroidery pattern is applied to the center of the fabric that you will be stitching on. Preparing the fabric will help you center the pattern evenly. First, press the fabric smooth with an iron. Then, fold it in half across the width and crease it with the palm of your hand all along the fold. Now, fold it in half lengthwise and crease again in the same way. These creases will create guide marks to help you position the transfer in the center of the fabric (or off-center, if required).

Transferring the Printed Patterns

To use the printed patterns in this book, trace or photocopy your chosen pattern onto a piece of thin paper. Place the copied pattern right side up on a table and tape it in place. Position the fabric on top, right side up. Lightly trace the pattern onto the fabric, using a soft pencil or a soluble- or disappearing-ink fabric marker. If it is difficult to see through the fabric, it might help to use a lightbox or hold the fabric up to a window.

Alternatively, you can use an iron-on transfer pencil or photocopy the design onto a fusible wash-away product such as Wash-Away Stitch Stabilizer (by C&T Publishing). Always refer to the manufacturer's instructions to use the product. Please be aware that some transfer methods will produce a design the reverse of that shown in some projects. Your project will be just as nice either way. However, be aware of designs that have words in them, or other designs such as a book that opens right to left, to be sure your transfer method does not reverse the design. Also, if the design is reversed, some embroidery references in the instructions may then be reversed. Always refer to the project photo for clarification.

NOTE

For a few projects in this book, the pattern is placed off-center; please refer to the individual project instructions for placement guidance.

Hoops

Excerpted from *S Is for Stitch* by Kristyne Czepuryk

To hoop or not to hoop, that is the question.

I'm comfortable with or without a hoop for continuous stitches, but I tend to favor without because I can control my stitches better and it's just more comfortable for my hands. Some people prefer to hold a hoop rather than limp cloth.

Continuous stitches can be completed by passing the needle from front to back in one movement. For example, a stem or backstitch is completed with a down-up movement of the needle before pulling the floss through the fabric.

But I prefer to use a hoop for stab stitches because I need another hand to stabilize my fabric while I'm wrapping floss around the needle for knots or for aiming my needle accurately.

Stab stitches are made by passing the needle completely through the fabric in one direction at a time. For example, colonial knots and the satin stitch are made by pulling the needle through to the top side of your fabric and then pushing the needle through the fabric to the back. In other words, two stabs equal one completed stitch.

When I use a hoop, I wrap a strip of muslin around the inner hoop to make it a little gentler on my embroidery fabric.

I wrap inner ring with ¾˝-wide strip of unbleached muslin.

Embroidery Stitches

Backstitch

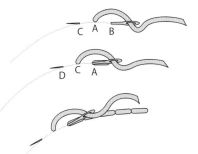

Bullion Knot

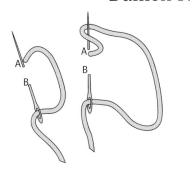

Butterfly Chain Stitch

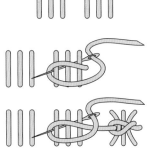

Buttonhole Stitch

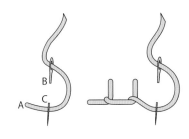

Chain Stitch

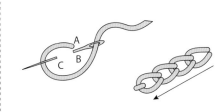

Colonial Knot

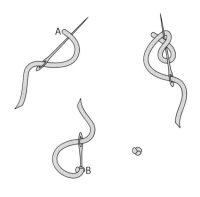

Cretan Stitch

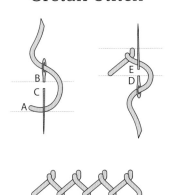

Cross-Stitch

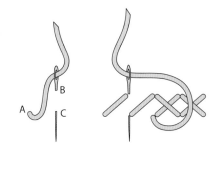

Feather Stitch

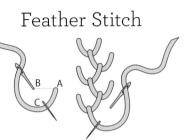

Fern Stitch

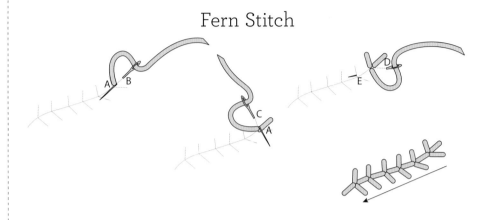

Fly Stitch

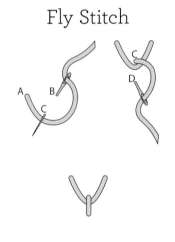

French Knot

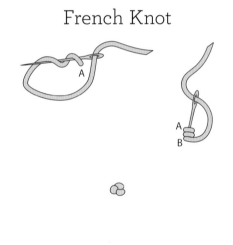

Herringbone Stitch

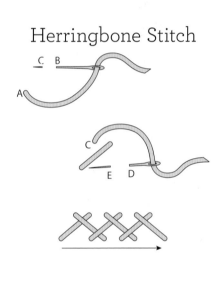

Lazy Daisy Stitch

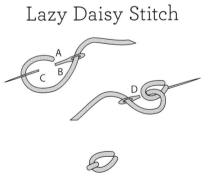

Running Stitch

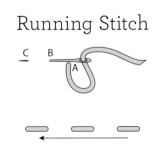

Satin Stitch

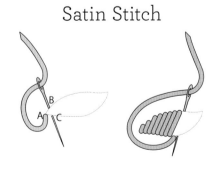

Seed Stitch

Sheaf Stitch

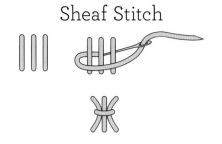

Split Stitch

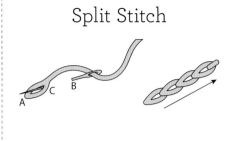

Star Stitch

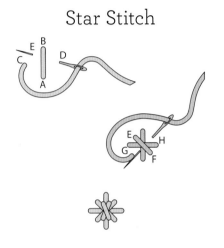

Stem Stitch

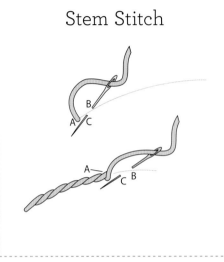

Straight Stitch

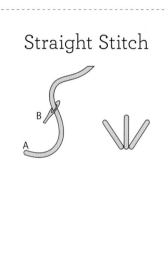

Tulip Stitch

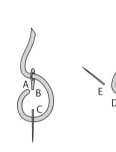
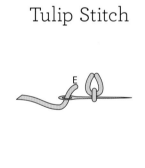
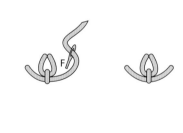

Wheat Ear Stitch

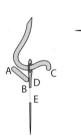
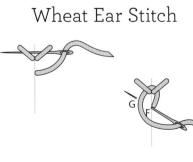

Woven Cross Stitch

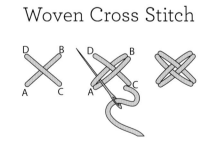

Binding Basics

Trim excess batting and backing even with the edges of the quilt top.

Double-Fold Straight-Grain Binding

If you want a ¼˝ finished binding, cut the binding strips 2˝ wide and piece them together with diagonal seams to make a continuous binding strip. Trim the seam allowance to ¼˝. Press the seams open.

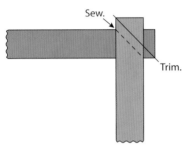

Sew from corner to corner.

Completed diagonal seam

Press the entire strip in half lengthwise with wrong sides together. With raw edges even, pin the binding to the front edge of the quilt a few inches away from a corner, and leave the first few inches of the binding unattached. Start sewing, using a ¼˝ seam allowance.

Stop ¼˝ away from the first corner (see Step 1) and backstitch one stitch. Lift the presser foot and needle. Rotate the quilt one-quarter turn. Fold the binding at a right angle so it extends straight above the quilt and the fold forms a 45° angle in the corner (see Step 2). Then bring the binding strip down even with the edge of the quilt (see Step 3). Begin sewing at the folded edge. Repeat in the same manner at all the corners.

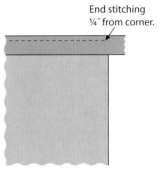

Step 1. Stitch to ¼˝ from corner.

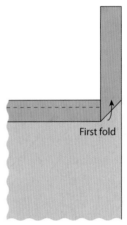

Step 2. First fold for miter

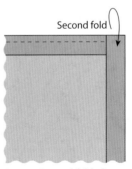

Step 3. Second fold alignment

Continue stitching until you are back near the beginning of the binding strip. See Finishing the Binding Ends for tips on finishing and hiding the raw edges of the ends of the binding.

Finishing the Binding Ends

Method 1

After stitching around the quilt, fold under the beginning tail of the binding strip ¼″ so that the raw edge will be inside the binding after it is turned to the back of the quilt. Place the end tail of the binding strip over the beginning folded end. Continue to attach the binding and stitch slightly beyond the starting stitches. Trim the excess binding. Fold the binding over the raw edges to the quilt back and hand stitch, mitering the corners.

Method 2

See the tip "Completing a Binding with an Invisible Seam" at ctpub.com in the Quiltmaking Basics section under Consumer Resources.

Fold the ending tail of the binding back on itself where it meets the beginning binding tail. From the fold, measure and mark the cut width of the binding strip. Cut the ending binding tail to this measurement. For example, if your binding is cut 2⅛″ wide, measure from the fold on the ending tail of the binding 2⅛″ and cut the binding tail to this length.

Open both tails. Place one tail on top of the other tail at right angles, right sides together. Mark a diagonal line from corner to corner and stitch on the line. Check that you've done it correctly and that the binding fits the quilt; then trim the seam allowance to ¼″. Press open.

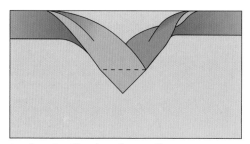

Stitch ends of binding diagonally.

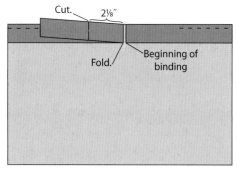

Cut binding tail.

Refold the binding and stitch this binding section in place on the quilt. Fold the binding over the raw edges to the quilt back and hand stitch.

Template Patterns

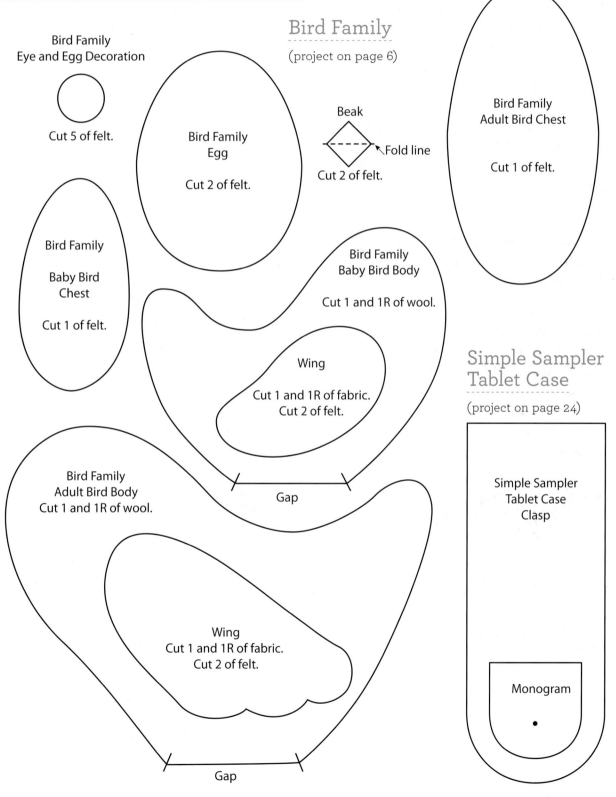

Bird Family
Eye and Egg Decoration

Cut 5 of felt.

Bird Family

(project on page 6)

Bird Family
Egg

Cut 2 of felt.

Beak

Fold line

Cut 2 of felt.

Bird Family
Adult Bird Chest

Cut 1 of felt.

Bird Family

Baby Bird
Chest

Cut 1 of felt.

Bird Family
Baby Bird Body

Cut 1 and 1R of wool.

Wing

Cut 1 and 1R of fabric.
Cut 2 of felt.

Simple Sampler
Tablet Case

(project on page 24)

Gap

Bird Family
Adult Bird Body
Cut 1 and 1R of wool.

Simple Sampler
Tablet Case
Clasp

Wing
Cut 1 and 1R of fabric.
Cut 2 of felt.

Monogram

Gap

Animal Antics Bib and More

(project on page 96)

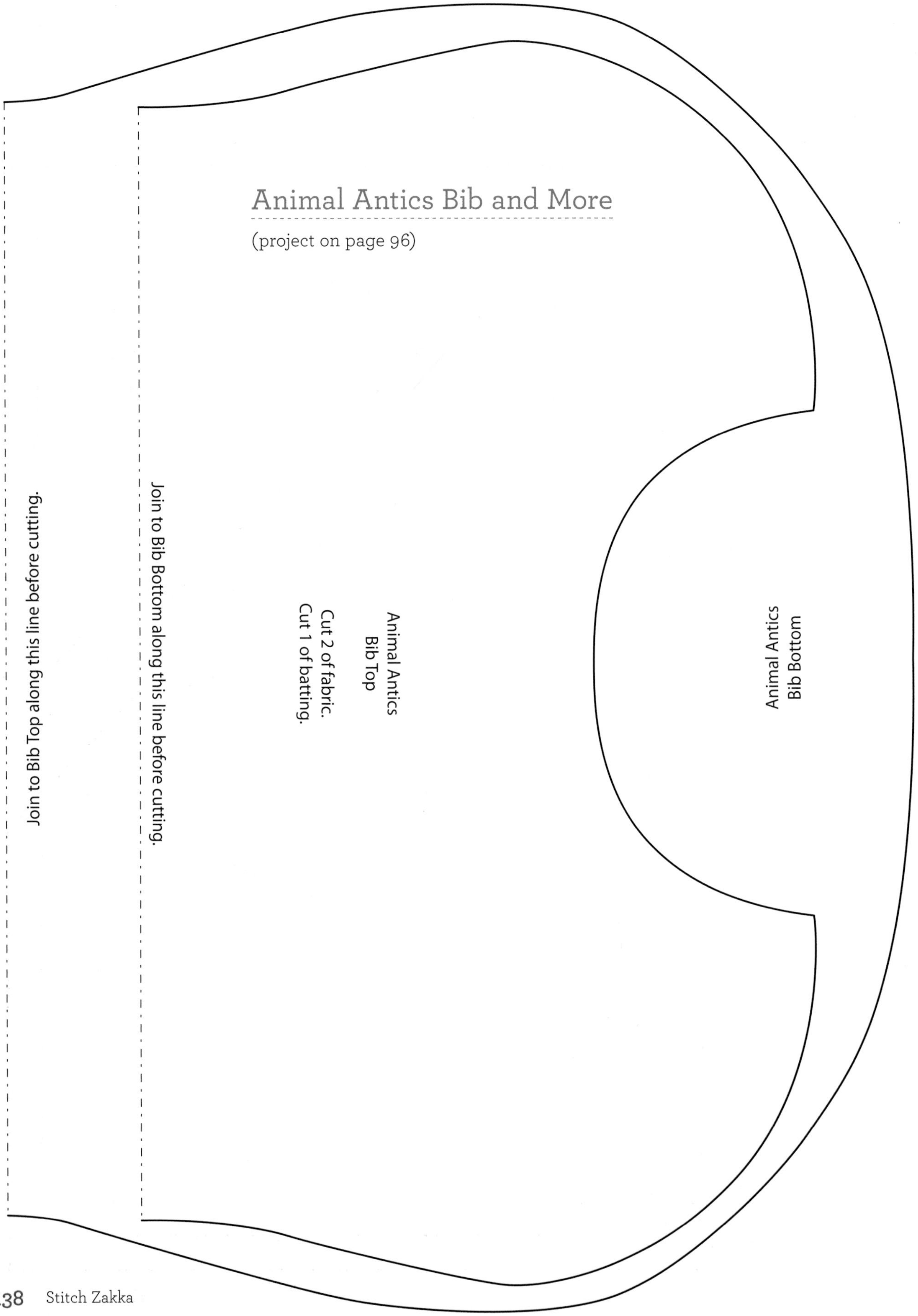

Join to Bib Top along this line before cutting.

Join to Bib Bottom along this line before cutting.

Animal Antics
Bib Top

Cut 2 of fabric.
Cut 1 of batting.

Animal Antics
Bib Bottom

Homespun
Needle Case
and Scissor Keeper

(project on page 10)

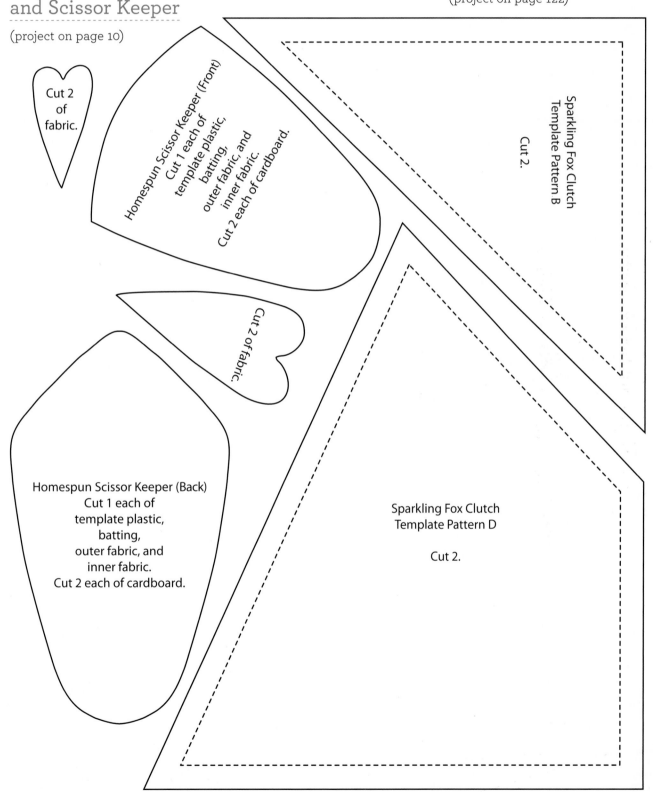

Cut 2
of
fabric.

Homespun Scissor Keeper (Front)
Cut 1 each of
template plastic,
batting,
outer fabric, and
inner fabric.
Cut 2 each of cardboard.

Cut 2 of fabric.

Homespun Scissor Keeper (Back)
Cut 1 each of
template plastic,
batting,
outer fabric, and
inner fabric.
Cut 2 each of cardboard.

Sparkling Fox Clutch

(project on page 122)

Sparkling Fox Clutch
Template Pattern B

Cut 2.

Sparkling Fox Clutch
Template Pattern D

Cut 2.

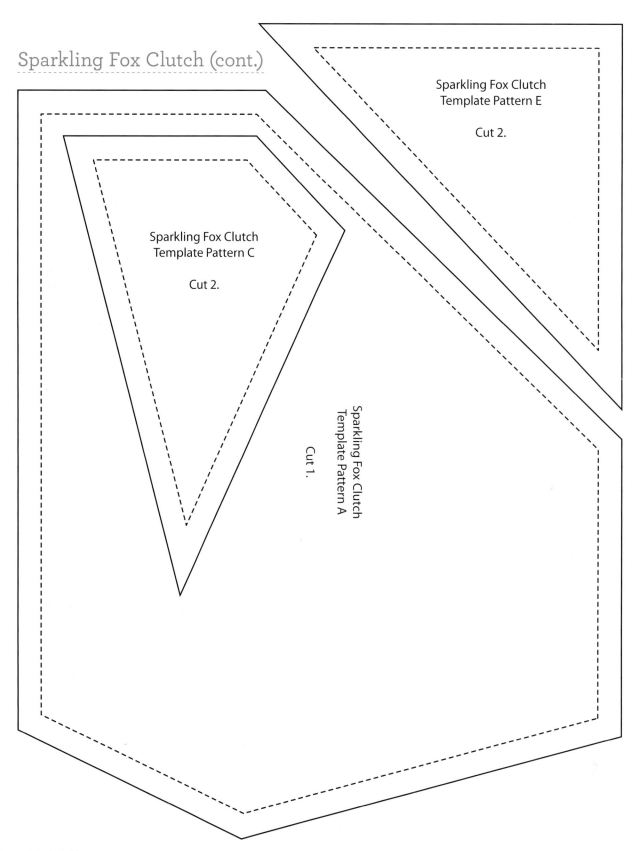

Sparkling Fox Clutch
Template Pattern E

Cut 2.

Sparkling Fox Clutch
Template Pattern C

Cut 2.

Sparkling Fox Clutch
Template Pattern A

Cut 1.

Contributors

Amy Adams is a UK-based textile artist specializing in designing and making softies from an ever-increasing portfolio of patterns under the brand name Lucykate Crafts. These softies are available as unique pieces, with many also featured as published patterns. Her work mixes vintage and recycled fabrics—in particular, felted wool mixed with hand-stitched embroidery.
lucykatecrafts.blogspot.com

Lynette Anderson's sophisticated yet naive design style is instantly recognizable. When she is not traveling and teaching, she works from her beachside design studio on Queensland's Sunshine Coast in Australia, where she opened Little Quilt Store in 2012. The invitation to join the team at Lecien in 2010 fulfilled her dream of fabric design. Her fourth book, *Stitch It for Spring*, published by David & Charles (F&W Media), follows *It's Quilting Cats and Dogs*, *Country Cottage Quilting*, and *Stitch It for Christmas*.
lynetteandersondesigns.com.au

Leanne Beasley's *Vignette* magazine, patterns, books, blog, and teaching are all full of her photography, little drawings, hints, tips, recipes, and other creative ideas for everyday life. Her main objective is to inspire other women to express their own creativity in their homes and lives and to really enjoy doing it. While basing herself at her home in Australia, Leanne also travels the world teaching, hosting travel retreats, and journaling the entire adventure.
leanneshouse.typepad.com

Kristyne Czepuryk was taught how to use a needle and thread at a very young age by her mom and aunt. When she was about 12 years old her attention turned to embroidery. She dabbled a little in this traditional art but then left it alone for a few decades. When she turned 40, she found herself returning to this timeless ritual of embellishing quilts with beautiful stitches and colorful threads. She wonders why it took her so long to rekindle her friendship with embroidery.
prettybyhand.com

Jasonda Desmond is a freelance graphic designer. Her design studio, Dotty Logic, offers surface designs for licensing, as well as illustration and identity-design services. She lives in Vancouver, British Columbia, with her husband and their dog, Rosie.
dottylogic.com

Jill Hamor grew up in Southern California loving animals, drawing prolifically, and playing soccer with her sisters and brother. Jill is a newcomer to handcrafting, having been inspired to design, sew, and knit for her three daughters, nieces, and nephews over the past nine years. More of her cute style can be seen in her book *Storybook Toys*, published by Stash Books. She now resides in the San Francisco Bay Area with her family and their black lab mix, Lily. You can find more of Jill's work at her blog.
bybido.blogspot.com

Aneela Hoey is a fabric designer for Moda and also creates her own quilt and embroidery patterns. She is the author of *Little Stitches: 100+ Sweet Embroidery Designs*, published by Stash Books. Her work has appeared in other books and numerous magazines as well. She also writes a popular blog. Aneela lives in the UK with her husband and two young daughters.
comfortstitching.typepad.co.uk

Mollie Johanson, a trained graphic designer specializing in print projects, began her blog, Wild Olive, as an outlet for more whimsical works. Daily dreaming and doodling have resulted in a variety of embroidery and paper projects, most featuring simple, expressive faces. Mollie, based in a far western suburb of Chicago, commutes daily to her in-home studio via the coffee pot. wildolive.blogspot.com

Robin Kingsley has been indulging in needlework of some kind or another forever. Now needlework, in the form of Bird Brain Designs, has become a terrific livelihood for her and her sister, Tina. The Bird Brain Designs Studio is in an old dime store built in 1937 on Main Street in quaint little Kelseyville, California. Every day is fun, though sometimes quite hectic, as the sisters plan new designs, stitch models, and make up patterns and kits to sell in the shop, on their website, and at quilt shows. birdbraindesigns.net

Natalie Lymer is a fabric designer for Lecien, a pattern designer, and the author behind Cinderberry Stitches. She loves combining her unique drawings with thread and fabric. Most of her days are full of sketching, designing, and dreaming big—her imagination and design inspiration coming from childhood memories, her little ones, and just simple everyday things around the home. cinderberrystitches.com

Charlotte Lyons designs and makes things to love. Inspired by traditional art and craft, she inventively repurposes materials to infuse her work with vintage charm. Charlotte designs fabric collections for Blend Fabrics, designs stitchable embroidery samplers for her Etsy shop, and teaches in national workshops. Her work has been featured in her books, *Mothers and Daughters at Home* and *Between Friends*; in the Mary Engelbreit Home Companion book series; and in numerous magazines. charlottelyons.com

Kaari Meng is a world-renowned purveyor of French living and the owner of French General. She sells vintage and new textiles and products in the United States, Europe, and Japan, as well as offering workshops and creative kits to people who enjoy working with vintage materials. frenchgeneral.com

Lisa Neal is the designer behind Lazy May, an online shop selling original iron-on embroidery patterns. She enjoys lots of different crafts but is a big fan of the quick fix, a little project you can start and finish in a couple of evenings—it's why she loves embroidery so much. Her patterns are cute and quirky and will, hopefully, make you smile while you stitch! lazymay.co.uk

Rosalie Quinlan has released more than 200 pattern designs through her company Rosalie Quinlan Designs and 3 self-published books. In 2006 she began a second company with her sister, Melanie Hurlston. They create fun and vibrant designs for quilts, bags, and softies under the label Melly&me. Melanie and Rosalie have written a book of patterns called *Sewn Toy Tales*, published by David & Charles, that has been translated into 5 languages. Rosalie has designed 3 beautiful lines of fabric for Lecien. rosaliequinlandesigns.typepad.com

Judy Reynolds has always been involved in something creative: drawing, painting, crocheting—just about any craft that came along. At the prime age of 49, she graduated from college with an art degree. A job at her local quilt shop changed her palette from paints to fabric and challenged her to create original designs, which developed into her pattern company, Black Cat Creations. It's never too late to live what you dream!
black-cat-creations.com

In 1985 Yoko Saito established the quilt shop and workshop Quilt Party. She soon garnered a reputation for precise needlework and developed her hallmark style of soft taupe colors. In recent years, she has held quilt exhibitions and workshops in France, Italy, and Taiwan. Yoko gives quilt design classes at several universities and at the NHK Culture Center in Japan. She regularly publishes books and designs quilts for magazines and TV shows.
shop.quilt.co.jp/en/

Loyce Saxton is the designer and owner of Yesterday's Charm. She started sewing as a child and hasn't stopped. She loves to sew and share with others. Her designs are inspired by the past and created for today. She believes we should have fun sewing and not worry about perfection—the joy is in doing. You can see more of her designs on her website.
yesterdayscharm.com

From an early age Kathy Schmitz had a pencil and paper in hand. Over the years, she's added a needle and thread to the mix, and by combining her love for drawing with her love for stitching Kathy has created a business designing embroidery patterns and fabric for Moda. She lives in Portland, Oregon, with her husband, Steve, and her days are filled with painting, sewing, and creating a home full of love.
kathyschmitz.com

Amy Sinibaldi lives in a small house by the ocean in Los Angeles, designing, sewing, and blogging while raising kids and cooking dinner, occasionally, for her very supportive husband. Hand sewing is definitely her favorite part of any project, and designing embroidery patterns is her new love.
nanacompany.typepad.com

Tracy Souza is the proud wife of an Air Force pilot and mama of two wonderful young people. She's been a creative "doodler" for as long as she can remember and learned to embroider in sixth grade. Plumcute Designs is the merging of those two parts of her. What began as a way to stay at home with her kids has blossomed into a more-than ten-year adventure that continues to surprise and humble her.
plumcutedesigns.com

Anne Sutton is the owner and designer of Bunny Hill Designs. She specializes in appliqué and embroidery, often bringing her love of animals to her designs. In addition to her quilt patterns, Anne also designs fabric for Moda Fabrics. She's been designing for more than ten years, and her work is featured in quilt shops throughout the United States, Europe, and Australia. You can find more of her work on her website, or you can follow her on her blog.
bunnyhilldesigns.com

Alyssa Thomas is an accomplished illustrator and designer. As a child, Alyssa made everything from beaded bracelets to large papier-mâché masks … to be bartered for at her "trading post" outside her bedroom door. Today she sells her line of lovely, quirky hand-embroidery patterns, kits, and sewing patterns through her company, Penguin & Fish. Her fabric collections are available through Clothworks Textiles.
penguinandfish.com

stashBOOKS

fabric arts for a handmade lifestyle

If you're craving beautiful authenticity in a time of mass-production...Stash Books is for you. Stash Books is a line of how-to books celebrating fabric arts for a handmade lifestyle. Backed by C&T Publishing's solid reputation for quality, Stash Books will inspire you with contemporary designs, clear and simple instructions, and engaging photography.

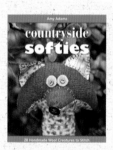
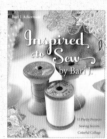

www.stashbooks.com